POISED

In Stilettos On The Front Pew

Wytress Mitchell

FOREWORD BY PASTOR BRIDGET HILLIARD

POISED
IN STILETTOS ON THE FRONT PEW

Wytress Mitchell

POISED IN STILETTOS ON THE FRONT PEW
Copyright 2015
Wytress Mitchell
BOX 682341
Houston TX 77268

Printed in the United States of America

Library of Congress – Catalogued in Publication Data

ISBN: 978-0692733325
ISBN: 0692733329

Published by:
Jabez Books Writers' Agency
(A Division of Clark's Consultant Group)
www.clarksconsultantgroup.com

Scriptural quotations are taken from various versions of the Bible and each version is cited.

All rights reserved. No part of this book may be reproduced, stored in a retrieval system, or transmitted in any form or by any means, electronic, mechanical photocopying, recording, or otherwise, without written consent of the publisher except in the case of brief quotations in critical articles or reviews.

POISED

Positioned *to*

Overcome Illness,

Stabilizing *my* **Equilibrium** *for* **Destiny**

FOREWORD BY DR. BRIDGET HILLIARD

It is 3:20 a.m. on Thursday, August 20, 2015. I just completed a 90-minute workout; while on the machine, I read the book written by my oldest sister: Minister Wytress Mitchell. To say I was inspired, intrigued, invigorated, and interested would only describe a few of the exhilarating emotions I felt.

Although she is the oldest of O.C. and Jewell Harrison's children, Wytress has submitted herself to my leadership. As a child, my siblings would always send me to get permission from DaDaddy to allow us different privileges because they always thought that if I asked permission, it would be granted. It was not until later in life that I found out DaMama told my siblings to follow my lead and always be there for me.

In this book, Wytress opens the eyes of every reader to the spiritual and natural fortitude it takes to live with a debilitating disease. Annually, as we embrace a new school year, I reflect on how saddened I was to know that Wytress could no longer physically pursue her passion educating young people. I am often reminded of the painful decision Wytress had to make to leave a career she loved so passionately to regain her strength and overcome lupus. Wytress, in this book, shares many of her personal experiences and challenges she had to overcome that unless you have walked in her shoes, you would not know.

To say, I am proud of Wytress would be an understatement. I am grateful that Wytress has found the strength to share her journey with the world. Wytress came to my office and shared with me what God put on her heart, and with much excitement, I told her to pursue this ministry assignment. I knew her ministry would affect millions in the days to come. I want to thank everyone who assisted Wytress in this journey.

There were times I wanted to be there and couldn't because of my commitments. However, I always prayed for God to raise up somebody, somewhere to use their power, ability, and influence to assist Wytress. Thank you for being the God-ordained favor in Wytress' life. My siblings, her children, and I are eternally grateful.

Finally, readers: get ready for an eye-opening experience that will encourage you to be poised. Wytress, you are indeed the healed woman of God! Continue to make God proud!

ENDORSEMENTS

This one is a page turner. You will not be able to put it down! Master storyteller and writer, Wytress Mitchell, has penned valuable insights on how to overcome a devastating disease... in style. She presents a good overview of lupus, including the symptoms and remedies. As you journey with her through the last three years you will conclude she possesses the fortitude to "consider not" and "stand therefore" until the will of God manifests. Her transparency will help you to understand how to anchor your faith in God regardless of how you feel or what the doctor's report says.

Wytress shares her trials and her triumphs, her tears and her testimonies in an inspiring fashion....in a way that will encourage you to maintain your poise... no matter what! As you dive deeper into this masterpiece, you will discover:
- What it actually means to be poised
- The importance of the Word of God
- How to release your faith through prayer and confession
- And much more!

Poised in Stilettos is not only a book, it is a life-changing process that educates, equips and empowers you to overcome all the challenges associated with lupus. Read! Learn! Do!

Josie Carr, Ed. D.
7M Stilettos Foundation President

As we approach the end of 2015, I am extremely proud of Wytress and the leaps of faith I have personally seen her take over the past few years. I have seen her transition through many life altering situations that would have caused others to give up.

Once diagnosed and faced with the reality that her quality of life was changing, she forged ahead in an attitude of faith and here we are today, with a very informative manuscript in hand that gives insight as to how to walk victorious and still remain poised - no matter what. She has walked through this phase of life poised in her stilettos even when the enemy would come in and attack her body.

Within the book, she very candidly shares the truth of every possible scenario experienced by someone walking through this debilitating disease. She also shares a glimpse of how even the assigned caregivers cope and offer aid to someone experiencing the devastating effects of Lupus. She helps us all to understand how to be more loving, compassionate, supportive and understanding when faced with a life-altering disease.

"Wy" (as I affectionately call her), you have handled every stage of this part of life as a soldier! I am extremely proud of you, and to see you walk through this season of life as an example of hope has brought me joy immensely. And as I've always said to you, "God has given you the ability to push pass this and maintain your poise!" I love you more.

Dr. Renee Fowler Hornbuckle
Sr. Pastor of Destiny Pointe Christian Center
Arlington, TX

Being a part of Wytress Mitchell's life and watching this book go from concept to reality has been a delight. "Poised in Stilettos" has been incubating in Wytress for years. No setback or health concern was able to abort this dream. Wytress remained faithful despite the way things may have looked to her. Because of her obedience, many people will be touched by this very profound message of endurance, strength and faith. One would never know what Wytress faced just by looking at her. She has always remained positive, encouraging, and dressed her best with her head held as high as her heels. While going through her struggles she kept a smile on her face and supported and served others whenever she could. In this book Wytress pours out her heart not only to tell her story which is very liberating, but she also stands as an example to help others experience God's healing power. I'm proud to be one of the midwives that has helped Wytress birth this book. Congratulations on a job well done, Wytress!

Kimberly Bady
Author of Authentically Me KimBady Enterprises LLC
Houston, Texas

DEDICATION

This book is dedicated to all of those who deal with lupus and other chronic illnesses and pain. There is someone who knows and understands the full effect of what you have or are going through.

The book is also dedicated to my baby sister, Andrea Harrison, who helped me cope and got me through one of the most challenging seasons of my life.

To my parents, who have both gone to be with the Lord: what can I say about those two? I will love them eternally. My strength to endure came from the knowledge and belief system you guys instilled.

Seeing my dad live with sickle-cell anemia most of my life gave me hope that I could also face my chronic illness with bravery.

My daily desire in my heart was my longing for my mother, Jewell, each time I hit a pivotal challenging episode during the various seasons in my life.

To all those who offered support during my time of crisis. To my three children (Lawrence "Jermaine," LaWrencya, and LaWrenette) who, together, helped me stay poised through one of the most difficult seasons of my life as well.

To my little sister, Dr. Bridget Hilliard: there are no words to even say thanks or anything else. Your thank you and dedication accolade is one that will encompass a whole chapter. Love you, dearly, Sis!

To my only brother, Reginald. Thank you for being there at every turn in the road when I needed a male figure. You rock! You were literally my shoulder to lean on when I could barely walk from the church parking lot to the front pew; you were there to help me stay poised.

To all the gracefully aged women, no matter the transition: bounce back, strut your stuff, and be poised.

Finally, this book is dedicated to you, the reader. Take notes, cry, laugh, gain insight and wisdom. Do whatever is necessary to stay poised! Be compassionate if it's a loved one or friend.

Wytress' ability to share her personal story reflects her strength to push past pain, isolation, and transition to stay poised. Her journey gives courage to help those who may be dealing with lupus or know someone who may be dealing with lupus or any other chronic illness.

Faith and prayer will bring you through some of the most challenging painful days of your life.

Be blessed.

ACKNOWLEDGEMENTS

First, I wish to acknowledge and thank God for His continuous healing power.

I honor and thank Him for using me as a vessel to touch lives through my testimony and raise awareness about lupus.

I am positioned to stay POISED.

Thank you, God, for your abundant grace and new mercies every morning. Great is the faithfulness.

To those people who taught me so much just by hearing their encouragements to put my thoughts on paper and eventually in print: Whether it was several years ago or as recent as yesterday, you were instrumental in the birthing of my first book. Two thumbs up, hats off, and a great big smile to you.

Dr. Judy Elaine Harrison, thank you for your words of prophecy even before I ever picked up a pen or thought about a book. Years before manifestation, you spoke those words, and you were the first to see in me what I didn't see in myself. YOU ROCK!!!

Dr. Josie Carr, you have been pushing me for years. You have always been able to pull my thoughts right out of my head. The best compassionate, classy, confident, and, of course, POISED boss in the whole wide world. There is absolutely no other leader like you. Because of you, I soared in life.

Dr. Cassandra Scott, I reached another turning point because of you. Thank God for the prayer line. I began to walk again when you screamed at me, "Rise...get up...Move your toes, now move your feet. Get out of that bed and walk." Thank you for trusting in me and giving me a chance to grow in my God- given gifts in ministry. Thank you for visiting me every time I was hospitalized from 2012 to 2014. Your words to me were, "Tell the testimony, Wytress." Every time I picked up a pen, I would hear you say, "Just write 30 minutes a night, Wytress. Get it done."

Dr. Sabrina Echols, your medical wisdom has helped me maintain my poise. During the miracle within a miracle episode, you came to the hospital, read the charts, and gave me the do's and don'ts of managing my illness. You were always looking out for me during this journey. No one will ever know how much you mean to me as a prayerful, compassionate medical doctor. You rock!

Dr. Renee Hornbuckle, what can I say? Like the perfect refuge conductor that you were, when I was going through the biggest challenges during this journey, you invited me to your home so I could heal after every major flare-up. You allowed me to vent, cry, sleep for days, rest, and rejuvenate. Thanks for all the healthy meals and your generous hospitality. When I felt all alone, you poured into me spiritually and physically. When I lost all ability to breathe, you shouted, "You have the propensity to push pass this and maintain your poise." You not only rock, but you also were my rock.

Apostle Jackie Phelps, when I couldn't sleep at night because insomnia had gotten the best of me, I had my own tailor made late-night private sermons. All of them started off with, "Girl, get out the box. Come forth, Wytress. It's your time. Let the ministry in you flow. This illness is just a distraction. You will rise and be poised again. You are my sister and friend in the city."

Kim Bady, you made me feel like I would be a best selling author even before the content of the book was finished. As my first book coach, you encouraged me in the early stages of writing about my journey of faith and healing. You taught me I could step forth and be unapologetically poised. You rock.

Cynthia Ross, you have been the epitome of encouragement. You always made me think I was a genius, and you were my cheerleader for every story and every testimony. I gained strength on my journey from you saying, "Ms. Mitchell, you are always poised."

Stephanie Hogan, thank you for always lending me your ear. When the book was just a dream and not a sentence was written, we talked about it and you said about the idea, "Astonishing. Amazing. Awesome. Go for it."

DaRhonda Williams, you planted the seed for this manuscript and the title. You encouraged me in style and to be myself. As the seed started from a thought, it has grown to something greater. I thank you for all you did. You rock!

To my nephew, Terry Egans: you lived that saying "If you need me, call." Not many can walk in those shoes. Even as hectic as your schedule always was, you were there for me. I will remain eternally grateful for your care and concern. You never failed to ask me how I was doing or whether I needed help with anything. You always made sure I had a way to church when I was unable to drive myself.

My thanks also go to the memory of Ms. Mary, who has gone on to be with the Lord. At the onset of my diagnosis, she always wanted to make sure I had something in my system (snacks, water and bananas were her thing) and she never wanted me to be dehydrated. To this day, I eat a banana every morning along with drinking a bottle of water. Not knowing she was going through a health challenge herself, she always looked out for me.

Stan and Dineta Frazier, thanks for caring for me when I couldn't care for myself. Thanks for always picking up equipment for me when I couldn't find anyone else to do so. Thanks for making sure I had a recliner during those days when my illness would flare up and I couldn't sleep in my bed. Thanks for being my personal "Meals on Wheels." Thanks for the couch, the socks, and the blankets. (Morgan is in Heaven now, but she's the one that stressed any women with cold feet should always carry a pair of socks in her purse. Here is a shout-out to Morgan.)

My Super "She-roes" Pastor Renee, Pastor Quette, Andrea, and LaTonya: y'all truly rock.

Pastor Trevon Gross, thanks you for your "mad" skills, because of you I have a manuscript in my hand, and in the hands of thousands to be blessed. You definitely rock!

Tiffiney Campbell, you came in on the very end of the manuscript, but, oh what a tremendous blessing you are! Only God could have connected us. You have a special place in my heart. Thanks for all your wisdom and input in every way. OMG!!! (My Daughter).

God will raise up people to use their power, their ability and their influence to help you. Again, I thank God for His guiding hand during my illness, and for the inspiration in writing this book.

PREFACE

Learning that I had lupus was devastating. As a believer, I had to pull myself together. I knew the Word of God, and I now had to totally rely on Jehovah Rapha.

In this journey, I found out that family members and friends might not understand the extended amount of support one might need when dealing with a disease as lupus.

I was clueless about every aspect of lupus and how it would affect me as well.

As you go on this journey with me, you will gain insight and be privy to personal situations and episodes.

In writing this book, I saw that I could answer some questions others had who didn't understand chronic illness.

Please read each chapter carefully and consider reading it again for added clarity and knowledge.

Once you finish reading, I hope that you will have gained a greater level of patience with friends and loved ones who are dealing with a chronic illness.

Some of the facts, tips, and episodes within this book are unique to me.

Although two people may be diagnosed with the same disease, no two people share the same experience through their journey. However, those dealing with any chronic illness should be able to relate to the core of the situations and episodes within this book.

Wytress Mitchell

TABLE OF CONTENTS

Chapters   Page

Outline 33
1. Jewell-ology 41
2. Causes, Effects & Symptoms 46
3. Fear of the Unknown 50
4. Before I Knew 54
5. Early Warning Signs 59
6. Graduation Day 65
7. In The Office With Dr. Bullard 74
8. The Journey 80
9. The Blanket 108
10. The Song 113
11. The Healing Word 118
12. Pastors On Point 153
13. But You Don't Look Sick 162

14. Dynamic Duo..169

15. Until You Have Walked..175

16. I'm On The Front Pew..181

17. Poised 183

18. Lupus And My Faith 187

19. Tips, Hints, & Insights 190

20. Gratitude Moments..................................... 200

21. A Message of Hope.................................... 202

    About the Author 206

*Below is the timeline of my journey.

EVENT	YEAR
Diagnosis & Rheumatologist	2011
Hospitalizations	2011-2014
A Miracle Within	2012
The Rebuilding Process	2013
Walking in Position	2014
Maintaining "THE" Poised	2015

Poised In Stilettos On The Front Pew

OUTLINE

Most people never take time to read the introduction in a book. Instead of placing one in my book, I thought I would outline what you will find in this book.

1. You will be better able to offer support to family and friends dealing with lupus. It will be a blessing to those who have little or no knowledge about what a person with lupus or any other chronic illness deals with. You will have more understanding, sensitivity, and compassion for them. There will be some strong "Ah-ha!" moments when you will inevitably say, "Oh my god!"

2. My testimony will set some people free and help them to get back their poised position. They will learn how to stay poised regardless of what happens. You will learn strategies to help you fulfill your destiny in spite of having lupus or other chronic illness diagnosis.

3. My testimony will show you how I managed to stay poised each and every day of my life. I will share goals and guidelines to overcome complications to live with lupus and stay poised. <u>Poised in Stilettos</u> will educate, empower, and equip you with the necessary tools to move forward.

Penning this book has helped me to be poised and push past the pain to my purpose: the birthing of my story.

The Birthing of <u>Poised in Stilettos on the Front Pew</u>

One Sunday in church, I was seated on the pew when I looked down and realized I was wearing flats. I had been through a major health challenge that prevented me from wearing my usual stilettos. I had to switch in order to stay poise and keep my balance. I had to wear flats.

My lupus diagnosis had caused me unexpected pain, resulting in a major fashion change. But how many know that although I was wearing those flats, I was searching for very cute ones? As women, our shoes define so much about us. Being poised and wearing shoes just seem to go together; thus, the story was born.

Shoes have always been a part of my siblings' and my life; not just my sisters' life, but my brother's as well. This little story will give you a glimpse as to why stilettos came into play and why the fashion statement was a phenomenon in my life.

You see, Harrison children did not wear run-down shoes or shoes with faulty caps on the heels. When you stepped out, your shoes had better be ready for you to be poised. From the time that we were young, my brother was always responsible for making sure his sisters' shoes were perfect and shining. We knew about the "shoe hospital" at an early age. In the Saddle Oxford era, we had the best-looking shoes. The edge sole dressing was to perfection and we had the best horseshoe taps there were. (Only if you grew up during the baby boomer years in an African American family are you familiar with this ritual.)

Throughout my life's journey, I went to many different events. I could always get my memory bank to pull up what pair of shoes I was wearing at each of many different events. Though I might not remember all of the details of the event itself, I remember the shoes that I was wearing. For instance, on the day when my symptoms from lupus took a toll on me,

Poised In Stilettos On The Front Pew

I clearly remember that I was wearing a pair of yellow suede stilettos.

A few months ago, my sisters and I found an old journal that my mom had kept about me. One of the main stories she talked about was how even at 18 months old, I was very particular about my shoes. I always had them in a certain place and I knew where they were. My mom's statement read, "Wytress is very particular about her shoes. She does not want anyone touching them or moving them. She already has about 10 pair and she organizes them herself."

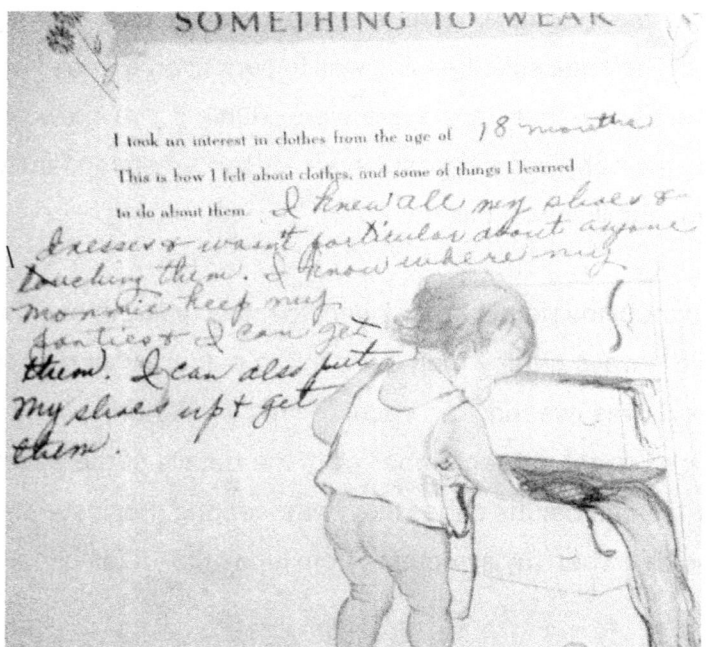

While dealing with the challenge of lupus, there were Sundays when I had to sit on the front pew not in my fancy stilettos, but in flats, due to the swelling and inflammation in my joints. Even so, the flats still had to be color coordinated in order for me to be poised. That in itself was a tad bit painful, because I really wanted to be poised in stilettos on the front pew, and I could only do so in flats. For as long as I can remember, shoes have been an intricate part of my life. This was not self-initiated; my mom, Jewell, had well embedded this interest into my spirit. It all started as a result of a dilemma she went through as a child. Her experiences as a child started the phenomenon of my love for shoes.

The story begins as my mom sat us down to tell us to enjoy and love shoes. She said buy as many as you want if they fit well, get them in every color. "A woman is not well poised unless she is dressed from head to toe and every outfit is set off by the right pair of shoes," she told me. "You see, you strike a pose, you strut your stuff, and you find your particular position and pivot, in a statement pair of shoes; thus, you will be poised. Let me just throw this in for image's sake. A well-dressed woman always has a little black dress, and a set of pearl earrings and necklace. She never leaves home without the right lip gloss on to compliment her outfit."

Moving forward in the story, my mom shared with me how as a young girl she only had one pair of shoes from the 7th grade through the 12th grade. You see, she had a stingy stepfather who would not buy her any shoes. Rather, he made her cut cardboard from a box and stick them in the shoes to make them last longer. My mom had to stand at her high school graduation giving her valedictorian speech while wearing shoes that had holes in them.

As a result of this experience, my mom vowed that if she ever had daughters, she would buy them all the shoes they wanted that she could afford. I was the eldest, and I was afforded all the shoes I wanted. As a little child, I remember choosing shoes over toys every time.

I was always poised. My mom taught me to always stick my feet out and be poised in those shoes when I would pose. Whenever we would buy new shoes, my mom would get in her car and start clapping. I don't know if each time this happened, she would reflect on her childhood of that one pair of shoes or if she was happy because she could afford the shoes for her children, but for her, it was always a grand celebration.

Even in the most painful episodes of my journey, I knew I had to get my shoe game right, because poise was a part of my persona as I stepped out in public. From these experiences, I chose the title of this book: <u>Poised in Stilettos on the Front Pew.</u>

BEFORE I LEFT HOME, MY MOM HAD ALREADY EXPLAINED SHE COULD ONLY AFFORD SHOES.

Chapter One

JEWELL-OLOGY

Some things from your childhood are faded memories. If you ask most adults to name the toys they remember having as a child, they can most likely tell you the name and color of each one. Well, I am that way when it comes to shoes! I remember everything about my first pair of shoes, including the design and style.

They were called Baby Mary Jane's and they were black, shiny, patent with a strap across the top, and they came in a little pink box! This was when I first fell in love with the color pink!

I loved those shoes, and when I put them on, I felt like a princess! Wearing those pretty shoes back then would be equivalent to sporting a fine pair of Christian Louboutins' in the present day. I even remember going with my mom to the store to get them. The store was Ballisteins, and as an African-American child back in the fifties, even walking into that store was a phenomenon. Everything about those shoes is forever etched in my memory!

They cost about $3.95, which was expensive back in those days. My mom had saved up to buy them for me. I remember the silver dollars and dimes she used to pay for them. For Easter, she saved to buy me another pair; this time, the white ones! This pair came from a different store: Foley Brothers.

Foley Brothers store in Houston in 1929 Photo: Houston Chronicle

Jewell Elaine Harrison. Mom, you were my jewel. You are my hero, my role model, and one of my greatest teachers in the entire world. Thank you for giving me life. You were absolutely the most brilliant lady I ever knew. If I can only be half the woman you were, I have certainly achieved much. I still make decisions in my life today based on those seeds you planted in my life. My uniqueness comes from you.

I saw you go through pain at different seasons in your life, and I was even there to hold your hand during excruciating episodes. I saw it, but I never experienced it. But through your visual directions, I knew how I should walk in this season to stay poised at every turn.

You left a mark in the universe, DaMama. By the way, I got a good glimpse as you were poised in your stilettos on your pew at Lyons Unity.

WHAT LUPUS ACTUALLY IS

Chapter Two

CAUSES, EFFECTS & SYMPTOMS

The cause of lupus is unknown.

Lupus: an autoimmune disease that affects organs in the body. It is a chronic illness with many faces. It can be a serious disease, however, it is not contagious. It affects each individual differently, but it is treatable.

According to the Lupus Foundation of America:

"Lupus is a chronic autoimmune condition that affects every part of the body. Approximately five million people in the world are living with lupus, about 1.5 million are Americans.

As with any chronic illness, symptoms can vary, and the on-again, off-again nature of lupus can be quite stressful. That's why many lupus patients find comfort in comparing and sharing with others who "get it." Often we find comfort in our fellow bloggers on the internet. These bloggers are full of inspiration and enthusiasm, and eager to spread a good "vibe."

One of the things I have learned on this journey dealing with lupus, rheumatoid arthritis is a disease that's similar. It is said, *"The most obvious similarity between RA and lupus is joint pain. Joint swelling is another common symptom, though with varying levels of inflammation. Both diseases also cause your joints to become hot and tender.*

As well, Lupus and RA affect your energy levels. If you have either disease, you might feel constant fatigue or weakness. A periodic fever is another symptom of both lupus and RA. Both diseases are more common in women than men.

Also, according to the Lupus Foundation of America, *"There is no cure for lupus, so patients are treated depending on their symptoms. Many people with lupus take corticosteroids and other prescription drugs to treat joint inflammation and pain. Others might need medication to treat skin rashes, heart disease, or kidney problems. Sometimes a combination of several drugs works best. People with rheumatoid arthritis can get cortisone shots to control the pain. Sometimes, patients might need a knee or hip replacement later in life because the joint becomes too deformed."*

Thank God, I still serve a God that heals! While I am not totally healed today, I still believe in divine healing. The Bible says by Jesus' stripes we were healed and this is what I believe. The Bible also tells us that it is through faith that we receive the promises of God. Therefore, I walk by faith and not by sight. I see only victory in my situation. **I am HEALED!!!**

According to Medical Alert:

"Lupus is an autoimmune (AW-toe-ih-MYOON) disease. Your body's immune system is like an army with hundreds of soldiers. The immune system's job is to fight foreign substances in the body, like germs and viruses. But in autoimmune diseases, the immune system is out of control. It attacks healthy tissues, not germs.

"You can't catch lupus from another person. It isn't cancer, and it isn't related to AIDS.

"Lupus is a disease that can affect many parts of the body. Everyone reacts differently. One person with lupus may have swollen knees and fever. Another person may be tired all the time or have kidney trouble. Someone else may have rashes. Lupus can involve the joints, the skin, the kidneys, the lungs, the heart and/or the brain. If you have lupus, it may affect two or three parts of your body. Usually, one person doesn't have all the possible symptoms but can."

Chapter Three

FEAR OF THE UNKNOWN

One of the most harmful effects of fear is the loss of your capacity to think rationally. Fear can be very stressful. It is very important to keep the fear factor from dominating your decisions when encountering circumstances that foster fear. You must learn how to quietly focus your mind, not letting the fear choke you during challenges times.

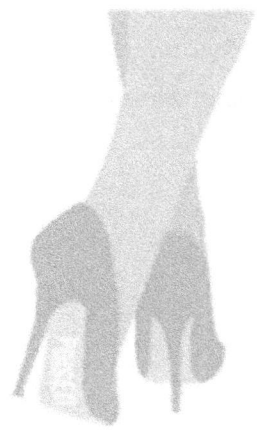

Not knowing anyone else with lupus, I didn't know what to expect or how I was going to deal with this major illness. I felt powerless.

When I was first diagnosed with lupus, I had to learn how to manage this type of fear. Initially, when everything happened, I had no idea that stress would cause my immune system to go haywire. And boy, I was stressing out about everything: my job, my children, my finances, my health, etc. As a result, the following season in my life was very difficult. I was feeling helpless, and my independence was being threatened. A big part of my fear was a lack of knowledge. What was all this medicine going to do to me?

How long would this last?

Not knowing anyone else with lupus, I didn't know what to expect or how I was going to deal with this major illness. I felt powerless.

{ PAY ATTENTION }

Chapter Four

BEFORE I KNEW

One day, I left school during my lunch break to stop by the mall to pick up a package. While in the mall, I begin to feel flush and disoriented. I became very hot and was short of breath.

I called one of the teachers to tell her to meet me at the door near the parking lot because I was feeling sick.

She asked, "Where are you?"

"The mall," I said. "I think I can drive back to campus, but I need to go to your room and lie down until I feel better."

I prayed for my health all the way back to the school, but upon returning there, I barely made it to the door. When I reached the door, I was very short of breath. I was exhausted and sweating profusely.

The teacher said, "Oh no, you are not lying down; I'm going to call your sister." My sister worked in the building across the street, so she was very close.

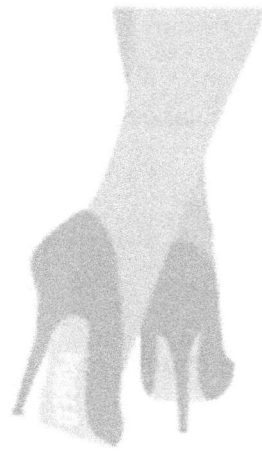

Because I knew to quote the Word in every situation, I begin to speak the Word over my body: "By His stripes I'm healed." I remember constantly saying, "Jehovah Rohi, be with me," over and over again.

My sister drove me to her building. To my surprise, my other sister was in the building, too. She came to my sister's car and said upon seeing my condition, "Call the ambulance immediately! Get her to a hospital!"

That day, I was terrified because I had never been in a hospital before, except when I had a tonsillectomy and when I had given birth to each of my three children. Each one of those experiences had been traumatic for me, despite being planned, so being told without notice that I was going to the hospital in an ambulance triggered all kinds of emotions.

Because I knew to quote the Word in every situation, I begin to speak the Word over my body: "By His stripes I'm healed." I remember constantly saying, "Jehovah Rohi, be with me," over and over again.

I was saying it so much that once in the ambulance, the paramedic told me to be quiet.

I said, "No, I won't."

He said, "Ma'am, your blood pressure is off the charts; you need to calm down and be quiet."

So I lowered my voice, but I kept speaking the Word. I believed that if I continued speaking the Word, then whatever was wrong would have to come in alignment for the good of my entire physical body.

The paramedics began to put I.V.s in my arm along with giving me some medication. I don't remember much after that, but I spent a couple of days in the hospital. They couldn't seem to find out what had triggered the symptoms and why I was feeling the way I did.

I had a follow-up visit with my primary doctor, but the symptoms didn't reappear at that time. After a few days, I felt better and went back to work.

A few weeks later, I noticed that I began to feel very fatigued again. However, I thought it was because at my workplace. I had been moving from one building to another, so I thought this might be the reason I was fatigued. This is what I blamed it on.

So I kept pushing because there was no way I could be out of work; after all, I was raising my grandchildren and they needed to continue on a steady course.

I continued on with work and life as usual. Every now and then, I would notice pain and a few aches, but I would take Naproxen and Aleve and just keep pushing.

Hint to the wise: Knowing what I now know, I want to encourage you to be persistent with your doctor and report all unusual symptoms when experiencing usual pain and aches. You never know when you are ignoring signs of a major illness!

As time went on, I picked up my pace and continued to push myself. Even though, I was getting more and more fatigued each time, but I never mentioned it to my doctor. Instead, I would rest on the weekend and just get up and go again the next week.

Lupus is difficult to diagnose, but there are early warning signs that can help you to get treatment sooner. Most illnesses are more easily treated when they are caught during the early stages. It is the same with lupus!

Chapter Five

EARLY WARNING SIGNS

I ignored them all.

I began to be late for work, as it started taking me longer to get ready in the mornings. One morning, I got up for work and I felt as if I was moving at a snail's pace. When I would get off work, I would go straight to bed and sleep until the next morning. I often felt sluggish, but I kept pushing myself, not knowing why I felt like this.

One morning, the unthinkable happened for a school principal who was responsible for opening the building. I got up to get ready for work, and I found that I could barely move. My back was hurting and it was as if I could not put one foot in front of the other without a tremendous effort. This particular morning, the students' parents arrived to school before I did, which meant they were sitting outside the school, waiting for me to arrive to unlock the building. Several teachers also awaited my arrival.

That particular week, I found myself putting my head down on my desk a lot. I didn't have any feeling like sickness, just general aches and pains. I felt fine otherwise. Other than feeling tired and sleepy, only my joints were affected, so when others questioned how I felt, I would always say, "I'm good." The pain was not severe; it was just annoying.

The only major thing I noticed was a reduced ability to move as rapidly as before. Being over 60 years old, I attributed it to normal aging.

It was the end of the year, so I had to push hard; it was time for me to focus on graduation.

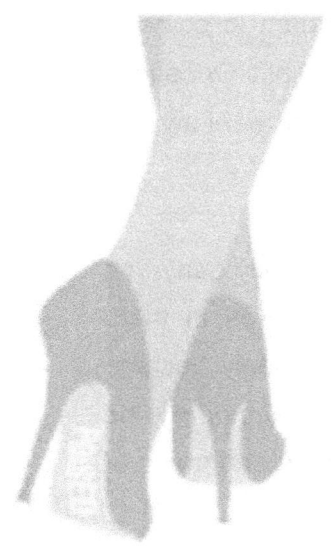

Weeks afterwards, I begin to feel joint pain again, my ankles would swell, and it became hard for me to open water bottles. Remaining poised, I continued to push myself.

One of the teachers came to me one day and said, "Ms. Mitchell, you look drained." She gave me some B12 shots, which made me feel better, so every other day, I would ask her for the pills. This kept me going for a while.

Weeks afterwards, I begin to feel joint pain again, my ankles would swell, and it became hard for me to open water bottles. Remaining poised, I continued to push myself.

It was now leading up to the Christmas holidays, so I took myself off the schedule. I asked my assistant to come in early so I could sleep late and work the late shift. Once I did that, it seemed that everything panned out and went away—or so I thought.

During the Christmas holiday, I got up unusually early one morning and made my way to Walmart. I was in there shopping for a couple of hours when I suddenly became instantly ill. It happened so fast that I was stunned by the feeling. Again, I felt flushed and experienced shortness of breath.

That morning, it was so bad that I slumped over the basket. Another customer came up to me and said, "Ma'am, are you okay?"

I said, "Yes," when in fact, I really wasn't. I became fearful because of the overwhelming feeling of being drained, and I did not even want to think of the ambulance situation again.

The lady kept watching me and she said, "Ma'am, can I call your husband?"

I turned to her and said, "I don't have a husband." She said, "Well, children or somebody?"

The next thing I knew, my daughter was there saying, "Mama, what happened?"

I said "How did you know and how did you get here?"

She said, "Some strange lady called me and asked me to come up here to see about you."

Thank God for cell phones. I had logged in my phone a note: "In case of emergency, call these numbers." My daughter was first on the list.

She said, "Mom, you were fine when you left home; what happened? Did you eat something? Can you drive home? What are we going to do with your car? Do you want to call your doctor?"

This particular daughter had 100 questions. I couldn't answer any of them. I managed to tell her to take me home so I could lie down, and I explained that I would be alright after a while.

Sure enough, I went home and laid down, took some Aleve pills, drank some tea, ate some soup, and drank orange juice for a few days, and I was all better.

No real episodes happened after that. Months went by and I was fine. I felt a little joint discomfort every now and then, but nothing major.

Chapter Six

GRADUATION DAY: MAY 2011

I had practiced with the children and staff for this day for months. We were ready to perform for the parents. This had to be the best graduation in history to date. The stage was set and the kindergarten class was ready to perform.

Of course, I was the principal, program coordinator, and executive producer of the production.

Poised In Stilettos On The Front Pew

It was my turn to take the stage. I was well poised and ready to show off my hard work.

This was my part in the program to direct the choir. Backstage, they called my name. It was time for me to make my entrance on the stage. I was hyped, ready to show the parents what their little graduates could do. This was the grand finale of the program.

I tried to bend down behind the piano to put on my yellow suede stilettos, and pain hit me in my side, keeping me motionless for a minute or two. The pain was so severe that I could not raise my head. Mind you, all eyes were on me, and the parents were waiting for this performance.

I proceeded to try again to put on my yellow suede stilettos, but my feet were so swollen that I couldn't get them on. I asked one of my assistants to stall the program for a minute with a few announcements until I got myself together. She did.

Finally, I was able to squeeze into my shoes, but the pain was horrific. Time passed and it seemed as though I was moving in slow motion. When I approached center stage, I had to pause. Once again, I had become overheated and had difficulty breathing. I pulled off that part of the program, but not without a struggle.

For the entire remainder of the program, I gasped for air. No one really noticed my symptoms, but I did ask for a bottle of water several times.

As the program continued, I felt sicker and sicker, feeling sick to my stomach and a tad bit nervous. I kept chewing gum and drinking water as I struggled to make it through the program without saying anything to anyone or alluding that I was in excruciating pain.

I made it, and after the last rendition, I immediately left the graduation. I would usually stand around and greet the parents, but on this day, I went out the back door, headed to my house, and immediately got in the bed. I felt so sick that I didn't even undress before getting into bed. I got into my bed and stayed there for three days. I was so sick that I couldn't answer the phone or even get up to eat or drink.

Finally, my sister came over. She had a key, so she let herself in. As she entered my bedroom, the first thing she said was,

"Why aren't you answering your phone?" I couldn't talk. Despite being under four blankets, I was shaking like a leaf on a tree.

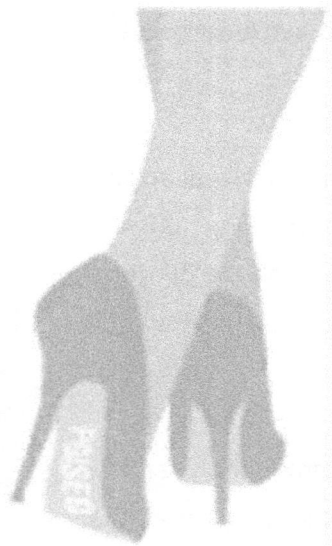

As she proceeded to move me out of the bed, my whole right side would not move. We all panicked, even my little Shih Tzu, who went ballistic because of how I was being handled.

My sister said, "What is it?"

Unable to speak, I just looked at her as she offered to take me to the hospital. I definitely did NOT want to hear anyone say two words: "hospital" and "ambulances."

I began to cry and then I shouted out, "No!"

She said, "Girl, you are in no shape to say no. You are going."

As she proceeded to move me out of the bed, my whole right side would not move. We all panicked, even my little Shih Tzu, who went ballistic because of how I was being handled.

The pain that day was unbelievable. I remember the severity of it as if it had happened this morning.

So to the hospital I went. Although I stayed in the hospital for one week, they could never pinpoint what was wrong. During this stay, it seemed that every symptom that goes along with lupus happened to me—yet I had not even been diagnosed yet. I stayed in the hospital for so long because every time I tried to leave, something else would surface. Eventually, I made it home, but three days later, I was back in the hospital again— this time for something totally different. I had broken a blood vessel in my rectum and was bleeding as though someone had cut me. I was kept on Morphine and other drugs to manage the intense pain. I couldn't walk or sit on my bottom for days.

After all of this, there was still no diagnosis of lupus!

I was in and out of the hospital for months; I personally began to feel somewhat like the woman in the Bible who had the issue of blood at this point.

In between each of these episodes, I would find strength to go back to work. I would get better with no symptoms and would work for months.

One day, as I was at work, I was walking down the hall and my legs gave out. I went to grab for the wall, but didn't quite judge correctly, so I fell. One of the students was coming down the hall. When he saw me, he yelled, "Ms. Mitchell fell --help!"

Some of the teachers came out of their classrooms and helped me back to my office. I sat there for a couple of hours with my head on the desk, trying to recover.

When the second shift came in, I went home. I did follow up with my doctor and, praise God, had not broken any bones from the fall. I was sore for a couple of days, but was able to return to work.

I went for weeks without any symptoms or complications. One Thursday, I was seated at the front desk when my doctor walked in. Her children attended the school where I was principal. She walked up close to me and said, "Ms. Mitchell, are you okay?"

I said, "Hm, my ankles are a little swollen, but I'm good."

She looked down at my ankles and then back into my eyes and said, "Oh no, this is not normal. We need to get to the bottom of this. What time do you get off work today?"

"2:00," I said.

"Be at my office at 2:30," said the doctor.

When I got to the doctor's office, my blood pressure was so high that she said, "You need to go to hospital."

I cried and said, "No more hospital visits, please."

She said, "Okay, but we are going to take some tests. I want to see you back at the beginning of next week. But one thing you cannot do is drive home! You must call someone to come and pick you up."

I called my friend Shirley. She took me home, prepared and gave me soup and juice, and then put me to bed. Before I could get back to Dr. Bullard's by the end of the week, her office called and said, "Dr. Bullard needs you to come in immediately if you could." I made an appointment for the next morning. And that appointment led to many more appointments.

Wytress Mitchell

> **MY WHOLE LIFE CHANGED IN AN INSTANCE**

Chapter Seven

IN THE OFFICE WITH DR. BULLARD

So there I was in the waiting room. Then my name was called to go into the doctor's office. When I sat down the doctor greeted me and proceeded to go over the stack of papers that were in her hand. I heard her say "lupus," and didn't hear anything else from that point. Every now and then, I would tune into a word or two. I heard what I should and should not do. Dr. Bullard talked about a series of test, and I heard the words, "You need to see a rheumatologist immediately."

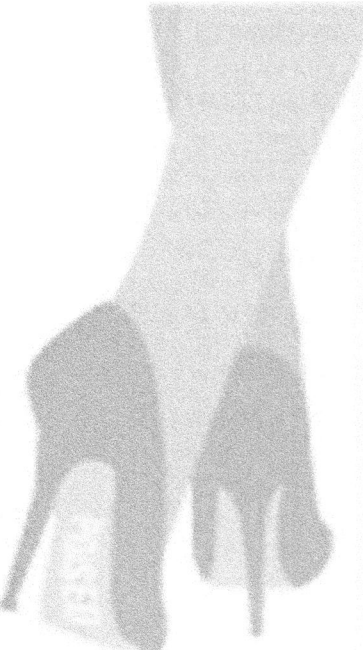

Rheumatologist. I had never heard that word before. As I sat there, it was as if she would fade in and out in the conversation. I would see her mouth moving, but could not hear anything. My mind refused to comprehend anything at different points of the conversation.

Rheumatologist. I had never heard that word before. As I sat there, it was as if she would fade in and out in the conversation. I would see her mouth moving, but could not hear anything. My mind refused to comprehend anything at different points of the conversation.

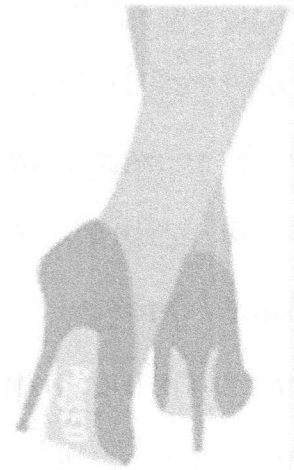

I had plenty of questions, but no words would come out of mouth to ask her anything. By now, tears began to roll down my face. All I could think of was, "What am I going to do?"

I had a blank stare several times during the conversation, and the doctor would bring me back by saying, "Ms. Mitchell, did you hear me?" I said, "Yes," but only heard bits and pieces.

I did remember saying to her, "This will be over soon because I have to get back to work." You see, it was the end of the school year and summer school had just begun; I was the principal, and any interruption in my schedule just wouldn't work for me at this point.

"You cannot go back to work at this time," said Dr. Bullard.

I had plenty of questions, but no words would come out of mouth to ask her anything. By now, tears began to roll down my face. All I could think of was, "What am I going to do? I'm in the middle of insurance transition and have no coverage for this office visit, much less a visit to a rheumatologist."

I knew that I should say something, but I was unfamiliar with the medical terms she was talking about, and I just felt kind of numb.

When I tuned back in, she was saying, "Your readings are off the chart. Your blood pressure is at a stroke level. Your blood clotting factors are way too high and your blood count is way too low. Your platelets do not look good. You must go home and go to bed immediately."

What did that mean? I never heard the word "platelets" before. None of this was making any sense. I talked to myself in my mind, trying to keep myself from having an anxiety attack.

I left the office with the papers from Dr. Bullard shaking my head. Although I took the rest of the week off work, I returned to work that Monday. I couldn't abandon my duties as a school principal. I had rested and taken the medication, I thought that I was ready to go again.

Not so. When I returned to the office on Monday, I went to the Human Resources department. One of my relatives was the Human Resources manager, so I knew it was just a formality. I gave her the papers that I got from the doctor. She asked me where I got the papers and whose they were. I stated they were mine and that Dr. Bullard had given them to me.

Because she had a nursing background, she understood more than the average human resources employee. She read the papers and had a puzzling look on her face. Visibly disturbed by her face, I quickly told her that that was last week and I felt better now.

The H.R. manager picked up the phone and called my sister. I overheard her say, "She is very ill." They both determined that I should return home immediately and go to bed. I did what they told me to do, but I still had a lot of unanswered questions. My condition wasn't contagious, so why was everybody all up in the air about it?

Chapter Eight

THE JOURNEY

Pull up your bootstraps and stay poised...

Here are some conversations that I would have with people while struggling with my illness.

"You're tired, you're out of breath; what's wrong? Are you okay?"

"Yes, I'm good, but my energy level is way down, I'm very

fatigued, this is just one of the things I deal with having lupus," I would say.

"Can you come and go with us?"

"Yes, as long as it's not too much walking. I can only walk so far without stopping to rest."

"You were moving around just yesterday."

"Yes, I was, and most of the time, a good day generally means three days in bed with plenty of rest."

"Do you remember this, that, or the other?"

"Ugh! Not right now."

"Why don't you know what I'm talking about?"

"Well, one of the symptoms I have to deal with is brain fog. If you give me a few minutes, I might be able to pull it up in my memory bank. But please don't get angry and frustrated. I'm trying really hard, but at this moment, I can't remember that."

"Girl, let's go out to eat. Where do you want to go?"

"Anywhere, as long as they have a good salad and vegetables."

"Why do you always say that?"

"I have to be really careful what I eat, especially when eating out, because of the hidden calories and the consumption of MSG. My body has become very sensitive to some foods, and I need to always be mindful of my diet."

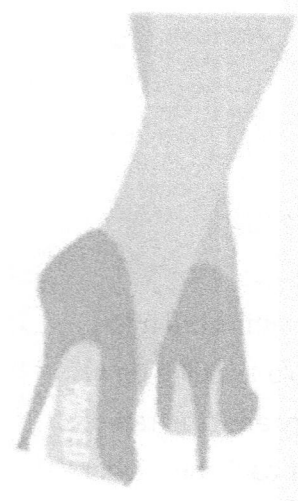

"Because it takes so much energy to cook. If I prepare a meal and there is no one else to clean up afterwards, certainly I will not have the energy to do it."

"Why do you have an electric blanket when it's almost 100 degrees outside?"

"Because if there's too much air blowing, my joints tend to hurt. The heat helps and makes me feel so much better."

"Girl, why are you walking so slow and why do you have on flats?"

"I have to be really careful because of inflammation: my joints are swollen and my feet are, too. But don't fret: if it's a formal affair, I have my stilettos in my purse, and when I get where I am going, I will put them on and I will still be poised."

"Are you picking up something to eat again? Why don't you just cook?"

"Because it takes so much energy to cook. If I prepare a meal, and there is no one else to clean up afterwards, certainly I will not have energy to do it."

"Why don't you just go to the grocery store?"

"Driving takes energy. I have to get out and shop, which is

more energy exerted. If I do go in and pick out items, I have very little energy left. Once I'm checking out at the register, I've zapped all my energy. Finally, when I'm driving back home, I have very little energy left. Who will take the groceries out and put them away? Many days, the items that don't need refrigerated sit in my car for days while I hope that I won't need them before one of my children comes by and brings everything in."

You see, the physical and mental fatigue associated with lupus can be overwhelming. Lupus causes you to accept and understand your limits. Diet is crucial. Unnecessary stress must be avoided. Tasks must be prioritized.

You must know when to slow down and rest, and you must pay attention to your body and listen to signals. That means learning to say no. I've had to reinvent what I was accustomed to doing. There is debilitating exhaustion, and the pain of lupus is excruciating, I don't think most people can relate.

Fatigue is so intense that you must lie down after any task. It can happen without warning -- sometimes, getting out of bed is a major task. When you have to go to the restroom in the middle of the night, the movement makes you feel as though you have run a marathon.

The journey began when my symptoms were so intense that there were weeks I couldn't walk. I would have to lie in bed until someone could come and help me move elsewhere. I would have the worst times at night because everyone had gone home. There have been times when I had to sleep in the bathroom all night simply because I could not get up from the toilet. I broke more tissue holders trying to pull myself up than I want to remember. Sometimes my feet were so swollen that it hurt to put my feet on the floor.

To have to make a trip to the kitchen to get a drink of water literally took me to the next morning to get back to my bedroom. My family quickly learned that someone had to stay with me at night. They took turns sleeping over. Most weekends, I would have a house full because we had turned it into a time for all of us to fellowship together. Each person had a task to accomplish to get things in line for me to make it through the next week.

During these times, I would sleep for hours with all the activities going on in the house. There were days things were so intense that I barely knew who came and went. My family members would set up schedules to prepare meals, clean, wash clothes, change my linens, walk my dog, run errands, grocery shop for me, and make sure my pantry was stocked for the coming week. My sister literally had to take over my bills because I was unable to do this task.

This went on for months. I had to be hospitalized what seemed like every other month. This went on from May 2011 until late December 2013. During this time, I had seen many doctors and it was as if we just couldn't get a handle on the symptoms and flare-ups. I was on a very high dosage of Prednisone and blood pressure medications, which relieved some of the symptoms I was dealing with. As a result, I experienced some relief.

A MIRACLE WITHIN A MIRACLE

As the weeks passed, I was able to move around and I began to drive short distances again. I gradually felt better each day. It was around the first week of November 2013 when I got a call saying my youngest daughter had been hospitalized. She had been checked in to the hospital and

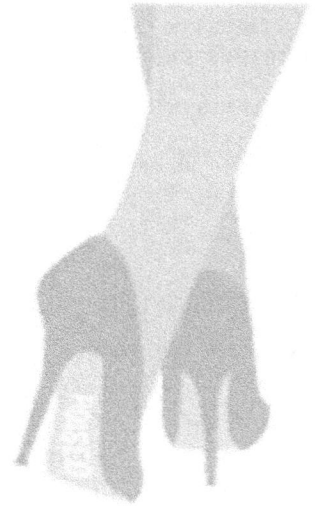

From the heavens, I pulled unbelievable faith and strength. I stayed day in and day out, never leaving her side. My own illness had gone into a type of remission.

moved to emergency. I stayed for a while, but then had to leave to meet my grandson's school bus. By the time I got back to the hospital, my daughter was in critical condition in ICU. She was hooked up to all kinds of machines, including life support. I fell to my knees and began to cry out to God.

I already had one situation going on with my health, but now my child was in a more critical condition than I was. I was told by her friend that my daughter almost fainted and was having shortness of breath. Only to find out after the doctors examined her, her condition was critical.

Daily, God supplied strength for me to endure this journey. You see, this was a 24-day journey of hospital visits and my daughter not waking up or breathing on her own, and I had to be there with her.

From the heavens, I pulled unbelievable faith and strength. I stayed day in and day out, never leaving her side. My own illness had gone into a type of remission.

The doctor came in one day and said, "Ms. Mitchell, you need to go home because you are not well and we don't want two patients in here from the same household."

I can only contribute the sustaining power and grace to the Almighty; Jehovah Jireh and Jehovah Rapha were in full control. For 21 days, my child was unresponsive. I called in all the troops. I had people all over the world praying both for her and for me.

Thankfully, after 21 days, my daughter awakened and began her road to recovery. She is a walking miracle to this date. After the day of her release from the hospital, I experienced a major flare-up. All the symptoms I had previously resurfaced, but this time to a greater degree. This flare-up was three times worse than ever before. I was in bed for months, and severe episodes kept me in and out of the hospital.

THE DAY MY HEART STARTED RACING

I mustered up enough strength to make a sandwich. I headed to the living room to bend down to turn on the DVD player, but before I did, I took a bite of the sandwich and pain hit me so hard in my chest that I gasped for air. I sat down on the ottoman to get my bearings, but got no relief. It was as if steam was coming from my nose. I began to feel very sick, and my heart was racing so fast that I could feel the beats with my hand. I was home alone and didn't know what to do. I had never had that severity of a heartbeat in my life.

I made it to the recliner and pushed the button to recline back, thinking the pain would pass. I was so hungry that day that I tried to take another bite of the sandwich, but when I did, all of the symptoms in my body increased. I got dizzy, felt nauseated, tears were streaming down my face, and I felt faint.

I readjusted my position in the chair and laid there for about 15 minutes, feeling panicked. But I knew something was seriously wrong. So I picked up the phone and called my neighbor Mrs. Berry, she said, "Call 911. I'm on my way."

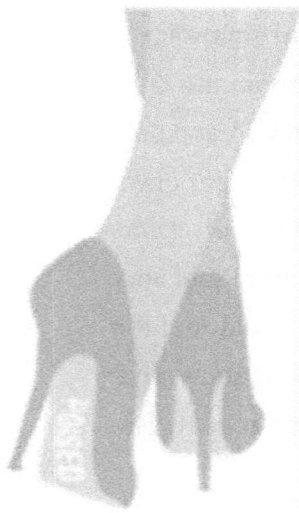

The ambulance driver explained, "Ma'am, we have to stop your heart and start it back." I freaked out… The paramedics still did the procedure of stopping and restarting my heart. That was the absolute scariest situation I had ever experienced.

The scary part was I could not get up to open the door to let anyone in, but thank God my recliner was positioned by the back door. I screamed telling the ambulance driver to come to the back door. When the paramedic team arrived, they immediately said, "Hospital. Your heart is beating too fast."

The ambulance driver explained, "Ma'am, we have to stop your heart and start it back." I freaked out. While I was in panic mode, Mrs. Berry arrived, and they explained everything to her. She began to pray in the name of Jesus, and that the Holy Ghost would cover me in order for me to calm down.

The paramedics still did the procedure of stopping and restarting my heart. That was the absolute scariest situation I had ever experienced. Thank God Mrs. Berry was there, because I had no ability to pray for myself.

Once in the ambulance, they hooked me up to all kinds of I.V.s. I don't remember too much after that because I was unconscious for days. I was in a state of delirium at times, and the only times I woke up were when the nurses and doctors came in. I was incoherent, drained, and very sleepy all the time.

After about a week, I was finally sent home with no real

diagnosis other than anxiety. I knew it was more than that, but because the symptoms didn't show up again, they said I was very exhausted and stressed.

Months passed without any other episodes of having a rapid heartbeat. But the flare-ups and the flu took a toll on me. I had severe pain for days. Weakness set in like never before. I would sleep for days, only to get up to use the bathroom and to eat.

GOD SENT A REAL LIVE ANGEL

My housekeeper went through a situation, and we both decided I could help her and she could help me. I offered her the chance to stay at my home for a few weeks to get things in order.

However, weeks turned into months, and then a year. God, was that ever a blessed year for me! During this time, it was as if she was my caregiver. She not only cleaned, but she also drove me here and there, prepared healthy juices and meals for me, and did everything else I needed.

Ms. Helen, you will never know what that season did in my life. I will forever be grateful for your commitment, unselfishness, caring, and going over and above for me. You stood by me and with me, prayed for me, and nurtured me back to health. For a season, I was poised because of you.

There were days when I was so sick that you took time off your job to stay and help me. You helped me to walk again, and gave me therapy without even knowing it. My house was cleaned to perfection and I never had to worry about anything. You were a lifeline in one of the most crucial seasons of my life. I was very vulnerable and you never used that against me. You were always so kind and trustworthy.

When the season came for you to move on, I broke. For weeks afterwards could not function. I would cry day in and day out because I couldn't figure out how I was going make it. Helen Williams, thank you!

THE SHIFT

In the next season, one of my children and my grandsons moved in. They were a blessing. God provided and I improved. I regained my strength and began to move around.

One day during this journey, the unthinkable happened. I went to pick my grandbaby up from school, and I could not drive once I got behind the wheel. I was halfway down the neighborhood when a sick spell hit me out of nowhere.

When I got to my grandson, he said, "Grandwysa, are you ok?"

I said, "No."

He said, "Pull over in the park and just sit here until you feel better."

Well, a five minute trip turned into me sitting in my car at the park for two hours. After that two hour ordeal, I was able to drive back to my house, which was two minutes away. When I arrived back home, I went straight to bed. There I stayed for two days with no food or anything to drink (My daughter and grandson offered me food and drink, but I was unable to consume anything.).

My sister came over two days later and said the famous words: "Oh, no, back to the hospital you go." I was not happy. My stay in the hospital this time revealed what the flare-ups were. Until then, I didn't know the term for them, how to detect them, or that I should pay attention to my body.

As time went on, I went through episode after episode. Each time, there was something new. During this season, I became allergic to virtually everything. Foods that I had been eating for years no longer agreed with my system.

On one of my feel-good days, I drank some ginger ale and grape juice. Within twenty minutes, my lips were so swollen that I thought they would pop. My eyes closed up, my ankles had become swollen, and I was a mess. I tried to get up and walk, but I could not move.

My sister immediately gave me some Benadryl and the swelling began to slow down. That was an unexplainable episode. From then on, I have learned to be very careful with my diet because on any given day, I may experience a new allergic reaction to something, whether it is food, drink, or some medications.

I had grown discouraged, weak, and very frustrated. Thank God my family was plugged into the life source, because they kept me covered in prayer. Every day, I got that phone call from Dr. B. in which she would say, "You are the healed, resisting sickness and disease." When she wasn't traveling, she would make her way to the hospital to pray with me each time.

THE NEXT EPISODE

One day, while using the restroom I had an uneasy feeling but didn't pay much attention to it. My sister came by to check on me. I was asleep, but when my sister awakened me, we both saw that my bedding was bloodied. Again, that same sister said, "Wysa, you have to go to the hospital."

As always, despite being teary-eyed and dreading the hospital, she made me go. This time, we didn't go by ambulance; she drove me there.

Upon arrival, it was discovered a blood vessel had burst in my rectum. This was an adventure in itself. At first, it was unable to be stopped. As a result, I needed minor surgery to repair it. What I did not want to hear was that I needed to stay another five days in the hospital.

By this time, I had grown discouraged, weak, and very frustrated. Thank God my family was plugged into the life source; they kept me covered in prayer. Every day, I got that phone call from Dr. B. (Dr. Bridgett Hilliard) in which she would say, "You are the healed, resisting sickness and disease." When she wasn't traveling, she would make her way to the hospital to pray with me each time.

Boy, did the journey get lonely and frustrating, but I had family and friends that kept me covered in prayer. My friends—Patrice Edwards, Dr. Josie Carr, Shirley Harris and Shelia Lewis—would check on me daily, bring me food, and keep me encouraged.

My brother would come to each hospital stay, check my meds and tell me what to take and what not to take. He was not a doctor, but was very familiar with drugs that could be addictive. Each time I was given potentially addictive drugs, he insisted that they give me something else, and they did. Eventually, I got better and was released from the hospital.

When I came home, Patrice Edwards brought me healing tapes from Dr. Creflo Dollar, and books and tapes from Dodie Osteen. After this, I grew stronger day by day.

I went through a period where I was able to move around better, but I still experienced severe pain and fatigue. During this time, I was able to go back to church and take short drives and short trips. This lasted for a while.

RELAPSE & TRIPS TO THE E.R.

One Saturday, I had enough strength to go to a conference by myself. Some of my friends were there, and we planned to go out to eat after the event was over. After the conference, I went to my car to make some phone calls and waited for them to finish.

While sitting in my car, I became very sick. I became overheated and experienced shortness of breath. I called them on my cell phone to inform them I wouldn't be going because I felt sick and would be driving home instead.

As I got on interstate 45 and headed home, I grew sicker and sicker. My heart started to beat fast as it did the day I had the episode with the sandwich. This time it was worse.

I prayed to just get home and lie down. However, as I approached my exit, my heart began to beat too rapidly. My heartbeat sped up until it was uncontrollable.

As I got to my exit, the Holy Spirit loudly spoke and said, "No, go to the next exit." I thought this was strange, but did not argue.

As I pulled around the freeway, I saw the entrance to St. Luke Hospital. I had been that way many times, but did not know that a hospital was there. It was as if the Holy Spirit guided my car in the parking lot and guided me to the right hospital staff.

The lady took one look at me and said, "Ma'am, let me take your vitals." She didn't even finish taking my vitals before I heard her say, "Stat."

A moment later, it was if I was surrounded by 50 nurses and doctors. They immediately rushed me to the E.R. I was immediately hooked up to all kinds of I.V.s. Two doctors came in and explained to me the procedures of stopping my heart and restarting it. Again, I was terrified.

You see, no one was with me this time. I had driven myself to the hospital. The staff kept asking me who was with me, and I said, "I'm alone." They said there was no way that, in my condition, I could have driven myself to the hospital. **But God!!**

This time was more severe than the first. The first time they tried the procedure, it did not take and they had to do it repeatedly. Again, the room was filled with nursing staff and doctors. The number of staff present in the room with me, along with my stress over the rest of the situation, spurred an anxiety attack. Although they tried to get me to calm down, my body was on "10" again. My legs felt like Jell-O and the pain was so intense that I could not lie still.

Finally, the procedure worked and they got me stable. The doctor said, "We will most definitely admit you, because we need to monitor what's going on."

I didn't know where my purse or my phone was. One of the nurses found it out in the lobby area and bought it to me. She said, "Your phone has been ringing and she said it is your pastor." (I have a specialized ringtone that actually says, "It's your pastor calling."). The nurse answered it on the last ring, it was my sister. She said, "I am on my way."

After several days of being monitored, it was decided that I needed to have a minor surgery. I needed an SVT (supraventricular tachycardia) ablation.

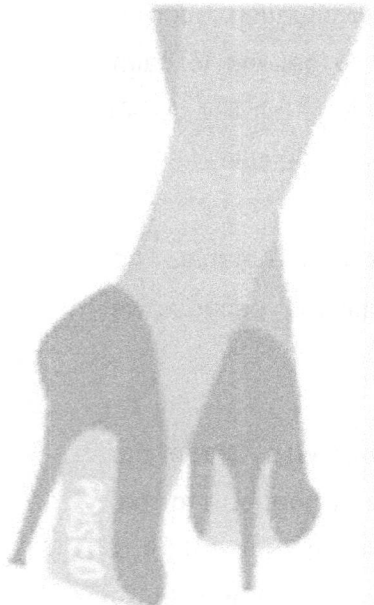

I had several more severe episodes in and out of the hospital until New Year's Eve 2013. Bishop Hilliard quoted the scripture, "You shall live and not die and declare the works of the Lord." With that spoken over me, I made continuous strides; after that event, I was able to pick up a pen and start the development of this manuscript.

This started another journey. Test after test, and a long hospital stay this time. In the process, I found out I was allergic to the meds they had given me so they could not do the test. The medication made me sick, which was an ordeal in itself. My tongue swelled and my throat started to close up.

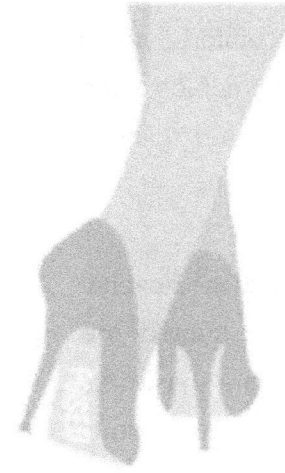

Although I live daily with pain, I consciously take steps towards being poised in stilettos on the front pew.

After this stay, I was in and out of the hospital five more times. I developed pneumonia and suffered from dehydration and flu-like symptoms. On top of that, the joint pain in my body had increased to a 22. Dr. B. came to the hospital on one of those visits and said, "This is enough!" She brought oil and did declare, "No more, in Jesus' name." She slung oil everywhere to the point that the nursing staff could not figure out why everything was so greasy.

Thank God for Pastor Robert Forbes and Pastor Laura Mitchell also. During some of my times of discomfort, I could always look forward to them bringing communion, and Pastor Forbes telling me I would be skating and riding a horse. That was the highlight of all of my hospital stays.

I had several more severe episodes in and out of the hospital until New Year's Eve 2013. Bishop Hilliard quoted the scripture, "You shall live and not die and declare the works of the Lord." With that spoken over me, I made continuous strides. And after that event, I was able to pick up a pen and start the development of this manuscript.

BACK IN A POSITION TO BE POISED.

Whereas I didn't share every episode through these excerpts, you can see a thread of faithfulness and God's favor.

Although I live daily with pain, I consciously take steps towards being poised in stilettos on the front pew.

As lupus is a chronic illness, I still experience unexpected bouts and episodes. I still have swollen joints, my blood count is challenged at times, and I still need to avoid the sun and extreme cold. I still must get plenty of rest. I still deal with severe fatigue. However, my faith is in the Almighty and *I will never give up*! I cannot go a day without Jesus!

Winston Churchill said, "Attitude is a little thing that makes a big difference."

Mary Radmacher said, "Courage does not always roar. Sometimes courage is the quiet voice at the end of the day saying, 'I will try again tomorrow.' "

You want family and friends to understand, but if they don't, then know that I understand that chronic illness is real.

Lupus is a chronic autoimmune disease that causes periods of flare-ups and remissions. A flare-up is best described as feeling lousy and really exhausted…pain awakening nausea.

There are moments when I get sad. However, I'm very proud of myself, because I refuse to let lupus get the best of me. If you want to live with lupus, then live!

I will not commit to more than I am capable of; knowing this has also helped me to live with lupus. My new perspective on lupus is in this acronym: L.U.P.U.S. is Life Under Pressure Until Success.

{ MY TOOLS }

Chapter Nine

THE BLANKET

First, I want to say thank you to Pastor Suzette Caldwell of Windsor Village United Methodist Church, who is the designer of the "wrapped in the Healing Word" blanket. Thank you, thank you, thank you. What an incredible endeavor! Like a young child who drags around their favorite teddy bear or a soft pink blanket, so did I with my healing blanket. There is no magical power in the healing blanket, but it was certainly a comfort to me.

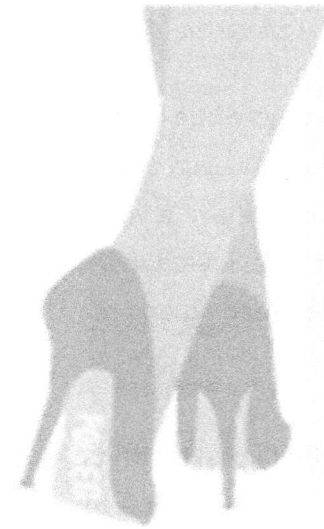

During my times of discomfort, there were days when I could not muster up enough energy to talk...But I thank God that I could use my blanket and focus my eyes on reading and re-reading the scriptures.

Every hospital visit, every trip I took, every transition from my sister's house to mine, and every night I slept in the recliner, I had my healing blanket with me. There were times when I took the blanket to church with me. I didn't take it to read in church because I could hear the Word there (I have one of the best teachers in the body of Christ, my Pastor, Bishop I.V. Hilliard). But I took it because it was so cold during the service that it would sometimes cause my joints to hurt. In order to be comfortable, my healing blanket would accompany me.

During my times of discomfort, there were days when I could not muster up enough energy to talk. I could not even get up to set the recorder. And some days, I just didn't have a voice due to sore throat and complications. But I thank God that I could use my blanket and focus my eyes on reading and re-reading the scriptures.

During one visit to the hospital, I was told that I couldn't bring the blanket in because of the risk of spreading germs. I emphatically said, "If my blanket doesn't come, I can be discharged right now." The blanket stayed.

The healing blanket became my comfort companion. There were times when I was in so much pain that I could not stand to have anything touch my body. Anything and everything hurt. During those times, I would sit the blanket on a table or prop it on pillows beside me so that I could constantly roll over and see the **WORD.**

Again, I want to say, thank you, Pastor Suzette Caldwell, for your brilliance of creating this blanket. It kept me constantly reminded of what the Word said about healing. With the blanket by my side or draped over me, I was always able to look up!

My eyes were always in a poised position to meditate on the Word, day and night.

JESUS, JESUS, JESUS BY PREASHEA HILLIARD

Chapter Ten

THE SONG

To my niece Preashea Hilliard: thank God for your vocals. Thank you for using your gifts and talents to bless the body of Christ. My testimony regarding this is very emotional.

There were days when my body was not lining up naturally. I could barely lift my head and stay focused. My limbs would not work properly. Inflammation was so bad that it would hurt to touch anything or have anything touch me. For over one year, I had retreated to my recliner, my blanket, and my computer (when able to operate it).

There were months when I could only operate one type of electronic: an old-fashioned CD player. Because of the way it was made, I had enough strength to press the "play" and "repeat" buttons.

For one solid year, I hit "repeat" from the time I awakened in the morning, until I went to bed at night. It was the song that my niece recorded: "Jesus, Jesus, Jesus, Something Happens When I Call You."

One day, my friend came over and showed me how to put it on my Apple TV. For that, I was grateful -- thanks, Matthew!. From that day, all I had to do was muster up enough strength to push the remote on the Apple TV, and the song would play until I hit it again to turn it off. When I would leave to go to a doctor's appointment, I left the song playing, saturating my house with inspirational music.

To my surprise, one of those days when I made a trip to the doctor, one of my children (who had a key) went to my house and turned off my song.

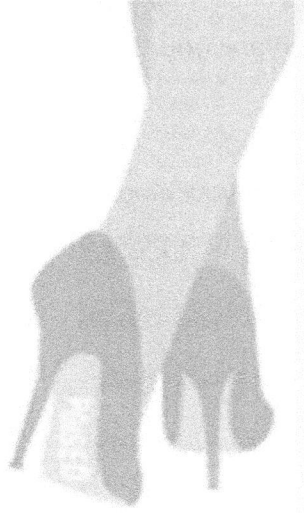

For that song, Preashea, I want to say thank you. As we once said in the Baptist church: "Thank you once, thank you twice, thank you three time. Thank you, thank you, thank you."…Your gift is amazing!

Later that day, I was told by that particular child, "Mama, every time I come over, you have that song playing. It plays over and over again, so I just turned it off."

Immediately, I sent out an email to all of my children and informed them to never turn off the music. I wanted that song to continually saturate my dwelling.

For that song, Preashea, I want to say thank you. As we once said in the Baptist church: "Thank you once, thank you twice, thank you three times. Thank you, thank you, thank you."

Your gift is amazing and the oil that flows from your singing. You have literally caused your aunt to come to a point of "STANCE" and be poised once more.

SCRIPTURES & CONFESSIONS

BY DR. BRIDGET HILLIARD
DODIE OSTEEN
PASTOR CREFLO DOLLAR

Chapter Eleven

THE HEALING WORD

When I didn't know what else to do, healing scriptures were my lifeline. These are scriptures that were used by Dodie Osteen, Pastor Bridget Hilliard and Dr. Creflo Dollar.

Exodus 15:26 Amplified Bible, Classic Edition (AMPC) Saying, If you will diligently hearken to the voice of the Lord your God and will do what is right in His sight, and will listen to *and* obey His commandments and keep all His statutes, I will put none of the diseases upon you which I brought upon the Egyptians, for I am the Lord Who heals you.

Exodus 23:25 Amplified Bible, Classic Edition (AMPC)
You shall serve the Lord your God; He shall bless your bread and water, and I will take sickness from your midst.

Deuteronomy 7:15 Amplified Bible, Classic Edition (AMPC)
And the Lord will take away from you all sickness, and none of the evil diseases of Egypt which you knew will He put upon you, but will lay them upon all who hate you.

Deuteronomy 28:1-2 Amplified Bible, Classic Edition (AMPC): If you will listen diligently to the voice of the Lord your God, being watchful to do all His commandments which I command you this day, the Lord your God will set you high above all the nations of the earth. And all these blessings shall come upon you and overtake you if you heed the voice of the Lord your God.

Deuteronomy 30:19-20 Amplified Bible, Classic Edition (AMPC): I call heaven and earth to witness this day against you that I have set before you life and death, the blessings and the curses; therefore choose life, that you and your descendants may live And may love the Lord your God, obey His voice, and cling to Him. For He is your life and the length of your days, that you may dwell in the land which the Lord swore to give to your fathers, to Abraham, Isaac, and Jacob.

Joshua 21:45 GOD'S WORD Translation (GW)
Every single good promise that the LORD had given the nation of Israel came true.

1 Kings 8:56 Amplified Bible, Classic Edition (AMPC)
Blessed be the Lord, Who has given rest to His people Israel, according to all that He promised. Not one word has failed of all His good promise which He promised through Moses His servant.

Psalm 89:34 Amplified Bible, Classic Edition (AMPC)
My covenant will I not break *or* profane, nor alter the thing that is gone out of My lips.

Psalm 91:16 Amplified Bible, Classic Edition (AMPC) With long life will I satisfy him and show him My salvation.

Who forgives [every one of] all your iniquities, Who heals [each one of] all your diseases.

Psalm 103:3 (Amplified Bible)
Classic Edition (AMPC)

Psalm 105:37 King James Version (KJV)
He brought them forth also with silver and gold: and there was not one feeble person among their tribes.

Psalm 107:20 Amplified Bible, Classic Edition (AMPC)
He sends forth His word and heals them and rescues them from the pit *and* destruction.

Psalm 118:17 Amplified Bible, Classic Edition (AMPC)
I shall not die but live, and shall declare the works *and* recount the illustrious acts of the Lord.

Proverbs 3:5-6 GOD'S WORD Translation (GW)
Trust the LORD with all your heart, and do not rely on your own understanding. In all your ways acknowledge him, and he will make your paths smooth.

Proverbs 4:20-23 Amplified Bible, Classic Edition (AMPC)
My son, attend to my words; consent *and* submit to my sayings. Let them not depart from your sight; keep them in the center of your heart. For they are life to those who find them, healing *and* health to all their flesh. Keep *and* guard your heart with all vigilance *and* above all that you guard, for out of it flow the springs of life.

Isaiah 41:10, 13 Amplified Bible, Classic Edition (AMPC)
Fear not [there is nothing to fear], for I am with you; do not look around you in terror *and* be dismayed, for I am your God. I will strengthen *and* harden you to difficulties, yes, I will help you; yes, I will hold you up *and* retain you with My [victorious] right hand of rightness *and* justice. For I the Lord your God hold your right hand; I am the Lord, Who says to you, Fear not; I will help you!

Isaiah 43:25, 26 Amplified Bible, Classic Edition (AMPC)
I, even I, am He Who blots out *and* cancels your transgressions, for My own sake, and I will not remember your sins. Put Me in remembrance [remind Me of your merits]; let us plead *and* argue together. Set forth your case, that you may be justified (proved right).

Jeremiah 30:17 Amplified Bible, Classic Edition (AMPC)
For I will restore health to you, and I will heal your wounds, says the Lord, because they have called you an outcast, saying, This is Zion, whom no one seeks after *and* for whom no one cares!

Isaiah 53:4-5 Amplified Bible, Classic Edition (AMPC)
Surely He has borne our griefs (sicknesses, weaknesses, and distresses) and carried our sorrows *and* pains [of punishment], yet we [ignorantly] considered Him stricken, smitten, and afflicted by God [as if with leprosy]. But He was wounded for our transgressions, He was bruised for our guilt *and* iniquities; the chastisement [needful to obtain] peace *and* well-being for us was upon Him, and with the stripes [that wounded] Him we are healed *and* made whole.

Jeremiah 1:12 Amplified Bible, Classic Edition (AMPC)
Then said the Lord to me, You have seen well, for I am alert *and* active, watching over My word to perform it.

Hosea 4:6 Amplified Bible, Classic Edition (AMPC)
My people are destroyed for lack of knowledge; because you [the priestly nation] have rejected knowledge, I will also reject you that you shall be no priest to Me; seeing you have forgotten the law of your God, I will also forget your children.

Joel 3:10 Amplified Bible, Classic Edition (AMPC)
Beat your plowshares into swords, and your pruning hooks into spears; let the weak say, I am strong [a warrior]!

Nahum 1:7, 9 Amplified Bible, Classic Edition (AMPC)
The Lord is good, a Strength *and* Stronghold in the day of trouble; He knows (recognizes, has knowledge of, and understands) those who take refuge and trust in Him. What do you devise and [how mad is your attempt to] plot against the Lord? He will make a full end [of Nineveh]; affliction [which My people shall suffer from Assyria] shall not rise up the second time.

Matthew 8:2-3 Amplified Bible, Classic Edition (AMPC)
And behold, a leper came up to Him and, prostrating himself, worshiped Him, saying, Lord, if You are willing, You are able to cleanse me by curing me. And He reached out His hand and touched him, saying, I am willing; be cleansed by being cured. And instantly his leprosy was cured *and* cleansed.

Matthew 8:17 Amplified Bible, Classic Edition (AMPC)
And thus He fulfilled what was spoken by the prophet Isaiah, He Himself took [in order to carry away] our weaknesses *and* infirmities and bore away our diseases.

Matthew 18:18-20 Amplified Bible, Classic Edition (AMPC)
Truly I tell you, whatever you forbid *and* declare to be improper and unlawful on earth must be what is already

forbidden in heaven, and whatever you permit *and* declare proper and lawful on earth must be what is already permitted in heaven. Again I tell you, if two of you on earth agree (harmonize together, make a symphony together) about whatever [anything and everything] they may ask, it will come to pass *and* be done for them by My Father in heaven. For wherever two or three are gathered (drawn together as My followers) in (into) My name, there I AM in the midst of them.

Matthew 21:21 Amplified Bible, Classic Edition (AMPC)
And Jesus answered them, Truly I say to you, if you have faith (a firm relying trust) and do not doubt, you will not only do what has been done to the fig tree, but even if you say to this mountain, Be taken up and cast into the sea, it will be done.

Mark 11:23-24 Amplified Bible, Classic Edition (AMPC)
Truly I tell you, whoever says to this mountain, Be lifted up and thrown into the sea! and does not doubt at all in his heart but believes that what he says will take place, it will be done for him. For this reason I am telling you, whatever you ask for in prayer, believe (trust and be confident) that it is granted to you, and you will [get it].

Mark 16:18 Amplified Bible, Classic Edition (AMPC)
They will pick up serpents; and [even] if they drink anything deadly, it will not hurt them; they will lay their hands on the sick, and they will get well.

Luke 10:19 Amplified Bible, Classic Edition (AMPC)
Behold! I have given you authority *and* power to trample upon serpents and scorpions, and [physical and mental strength and ability] over all the power that the enemy [possesses]; and nothing shall in any way harm you.

John 9:31 Amplified Bible, Classic Edition (AMPC)
We know that God does not listen to sinners; but if anyone is God-fearing *and* a worshiper of Him and does His will, He listens to him.

John 10:10 Amplified Bible, Classic Edition (AMPC)
The thief comes only in order to steal and kill and destroy. I came that they may have *and* enjoy life, and have it in abundance (to the full, till it overflows).

Christ purchased our freedom [redeeming us] from the curse (doom) of the Law [and its condemnation] by [Himself] becoming a curse for us, for it is written [in the Scriptures], Cursed is everyone who hangs on a tree (is crucified.

Galatians 3:13 (Amplified Bible)
Classic Edition (AMPC)

Romans 8:11 Amplified Bible, Classic Edition (AMPC)
And if the Spirit of Him Who raised up Jesus from the dead dwells in you, [then] He Who raised up Christ *Jesus* from the dead will also restore to life your mortal (short-lived, perishable) bodies through His Spirit Who dwells in you.

2 Corinthians 1:20 Amplified Bible, Classic Edition (AMPC)
For as many as are the promises of God, they all find their Yes [answer] in Him [Christ]. For this reason we also utter the Amen (so be it) to God through Him [in His Person and by His agency] to the glory of God.

2 Corinthians 10:3-5 Amplified Bible, Classic Edition (AMPC) For though we walk (live) in the flesh, we are not carrying on our warfare according to the flesh *and* using mere human weapons. For the weapons of our warfare are not physical [weapons of flesh and blood], but they are mighty before God for the overthrow *and* destruction of strongholds, [Inasmuch as we] refute arguments *and* theories *and* reasonings and every proud *and* lofty thing that sets itself up against the [true] knowledge of God; and we lead every thought *and* purpose away captive into the obedience of Christ (the Messiah, the Anointed One),

Romans 4:19-21 Amplified Bible, Classic Edition (AMPC)
He did not weaken in faith when he considered the [utter] impotence of his own body, which was as good as dead because he was about a hundred years old, or [when he considered] the barrenness of Sarah's [deadened] womb. No unbelief *or* distrust made him waver (doubtingly question) concerning the promise of God, but he grew strong *and* was empowered by faith as he gave praise *and* glory to God, Fully satisfied *and* assured that God was able *and* mighty to keep His word *and* to do what He had promised.

Ephesians 6:10-17 Amplified Bible, Classic Edition (AMPC)
In conclusion, be strong in the Lord [be empowered through your union with Him]; draw your strength from Him [that strength which His boundless might provides]. Put on God's whole armor [the armor of a heavy-armed soldier which God supplies], that you may be able successfully to stand up against [all] the strategies *and* the deceits of the devil. For we are not wrestling with flesh and blood [contending only with physical opponents], but against the despotisms, against the powers, against [the master spirits who are] the world rulers of this present darkness, against the spirit forces of wickedness in the heavenly (supernatural) sphere. Therefore put on God's complete armor, that you may be

able to resist *and* stand your ground on the evil day [of danger], and, having done all [the crisis demands], to stand [firmly in your place]. Stand therefore [hold your ground], having tightened the belt of truth around your loins and having put on the breastplate of integrity *and* of moral rectitude *and* right standing with God, And having shod your feet in preparation [to face the enemy with the firm-footed stability, the promptness, and the readiness produced by the good news] of the Gospel of peace. Lift up over all the [covering] shield of saving faith, upon which you can quench all the flaming missiles of the wicked [one]. And take the helmet of salvation and the sword that the Spirit wields, which is the Word of God.

Philippians 1:6 Amplified Bible, Classic Edition (AMPC)
And I am convinced *and* sure of this very thing, that He Who began a good work in you will continue until the day of Jesus Christ [right up to the time of His return], developing [that good work] *and* perfecting *and* bringing it to full completion in you.

Philippians 2:13 Amplified Bible, Classic Edition (AMPC)
[Not in your own strength] for it is God Who is all the while effectually at work in you [energizing and creating in you the

power and desire], both to will and to work for His good pleasure *and* satisfaction *and* delight.

Philippians 4:6-8 Amplified Bible, Classic Edition (AMPC)
Do not fret or have any anxiety about anything, but in every circumstance *and* in everything, by prayer and petition (definite requests), with thanksgiving, continue to make your wants known to God. And God's peace [shall be yours, that tranquil state of a soul assured of its salvation through Christ, and so fearing nothing from God and being content with its earthly lot of whatever sort that is, that peace] which transcends all understanding shall garrison *and* mount guard over your hearts and minds in Christ Jesus. For the rest, brethren, whatever is true, whatever is worthy of reverence *and* is honorable *and* seemly, whatever is just, whatever is pure, whatever is lovely *and* lovable, whatever is kind *and* winsome *and* gracious, if there is any virtue *and* excellence, if there is anything worthy of praise, think on *and* weigh *and* take account of these things [fix your minds on them].

2 Timothy 1:7 Amplified Bible, Classic Edition (AMPC)
For God did not give us a spirit of timidity (of cowardice, of craven and cringing and fawning fear), but [He has given us

a spirit] of power and of love and of calm *and* well-balanced mind *and* discipline *and* self-control.

Hebrews 10:23, 25 Amplified Bible, Classic Edition (AMPC)
So let us seize *and* hold fast *and* retain without wavering the hope we cherish *and* confess *and* our acknowledgment of it, for He Who promised is reliable (sure) *and* faithful to His word. Not forsaking *or* neglecting to assemble together [as believers], as is the habit of some people, but admonishing (warning, urging, and encouraging) one another, and all the more faithfully as you see the day approaching.

Hebrews 10:35 Amplified Bible, Classic Edition (AMPC)
Do not, therefore, fling away your fearless confidence, for it carries a great *and* glorious compensation of reward.

Hebrews 11:11 Amplified Bible, Classic Edition (AMPC)
Because of faith also Sarah herself received physical power to conceive a child, even when she was long past the age for it, because she considered [God] Who had given her the promise to be reliable *and* trustworthy *and* true to His word.

Hebrews 13:8 Amplified Bible, Classic Edition (AMPC)
Jesus Christ (the Messiah) is [always] the same, yesterday, today, [yes] and forever (to the ages).

James 1:5 Amplified Bible, Classic Edition (AMPC)
If any of you is deficient in wisdom, let him ask of the giving God [Who gives] to everyone liberally *and* ungrudgingly, without reproaching *or* faultfinding, and it will be given him.

James 3:17 Amplified Bible, Classic Edition (AMPC)
But the wisdom from above is first of all pure (undefiled); then it is peace-loving, courteous (considerate, gentle). [It is willing to] yield to reason, full of compassion and good fruits; it is wholehearted *and* straightforward, impartial *and* unfeigned (free from doubts, wavering, and insincerity).

James 4:7-8 Amplified Bible, Classic Edition (AMPC)
So be subject to God. Resist the devil [stand firm against him], and he will flee from you. Come close to God and He will come close to you. [Recognize that you are] sinners, get your soiled hands clean; [realize that you have been disloyal] wavering individuals with divided interests, and purify your hearts [of your spiritual adultery].

He personally bore our sins in His [own] body on the tree [as on an altar and offered Himself on it], that we might die (cease to exist) to sin and live to righteousness. By His wounds you have been healed.

1 Peter 2:24 Amplified Bible Classic Edition (AMPC)

James 5:14-15 Amplified Bible, Classic Edition (AMPC)
Is anyone among you sick? He should call in the church elders (the spiritual guides). And they should pray over him, anointing him with oil in the Lord's name. And the prayer [that is] of faith will save him who is sick, and the Lord will restore him; and if he has committed sins, he will be forgiven.

1 Peter 5:7-9 Amplified Bible, Classic Edition (AMPC)
Casting the whole of your care [all your anxieties, all your worries, all your concerns, once and for all] on Him, for He cares for you affectionately *and* cares about you watchfully. Be well balanced (temperate, sober of mind), be vigilant *and* cautious at all times; for that enemy of yours, the devil, roams around like a lion roaring [in fierce hunger], seeking someone to seize upon *and* devour. Withstand him; be firm in faith [against his onset—rooted, established, strong, immovable, and determined], knowing that the same (identical) sufferings are appointed to your brotherhood (the whole body of Christians) throughout the world.

1 John 3:21-22 Amplified Bible, Classic Edition (AMPC)
And, beloved, if our consciences (our hearts) do not accuse us [if they do not make us feel guilty and condemn us], we have confidence (complete assurance and boldness) before

God, And we receive from Him whatever we ask, because we [watchfully] obey His orders [observe His suggestions and injunctions, follow His plan for us] *and* [habitually] practice what is pleasing to Him.

1 John 5:14-15 Amplified Bible, Classic Edition (AMPC)
And this is the confidence (the assurance, the privilege of boldness) which we have in Him: [we are sure] that if we ask anything (make any request) according to His will (in agreement with His own plan), He listens to *and* hears us. And if (since) we [positively] know that He listens to us in whatever we ask, we also know [with settled and absolute knowledge] that we have [granted us as our present possessions] the requests made of Him.

3 John 1:2 Amplified Bible, Classic Edition (AMPC)
Beloved, I pray that you may prosper in every way and [that your body] may keep well, even as [I know] your soul keeps well *and* prospers.

Revelation 12:11 Amplified Bible, Classic Edition (AMPC)
And they have overcome (conquered) him by means of the blood of the Lamb and by the utterance of their testimony, for they did not love *and* cling to life even when faced with death

[holding their lives cheap till they had to die for their witnessing].

More Scriptures from the New King James Translation:

The Word of God will save your life.
Proverbs 4:20-22 New King James Version (NKJV)
My son, give attention to my words; Incline your ear to my sayings. Do not let them depart from your eyes; Keep them in the midst of your heart. For they *are* life to those who find them, And health to all their flesh.

God's Word will not fail.
Joshua 21:45 New King James Version (NKJV)
Not a word failed of any good thing which the LORD had spoken to the house of Israel. All came to pass.

God's will—healing—is working in you.
Philippians 2:13 New King James Version (NKJV)
for it is God who works in you both to will and to do for *His* good pleasure.

The Spirit of Life is making your body alive.
Romans 8:11 New King James Version (NKJV)
But if the Spirit of Him who raised Jesus from the dead dwells in you, He who raised Christ from the dead will also give life to your mortal bodies through His Spirit who dwells in you.

God is for you.
1 Corinthians 1:20 New King James Version (NKJV)
For all the promises of God in Him *are* Yes, and in Him Amen, to the glory of God through us.

It is God's will for you to be healed.
Matthew 8:2-3 New King James Version (NKJV)
And behold, a leper came and worshiped Him, saying, "Lord, if You are willing, You can make me clean." Then Jesus put out *His* hand and touched him, saying, "I am willing; be cleansed." Immediately his leprosy was cleansed. *Obey God's Word and be healed.*

Exodus 15:26 New King James Version (NKJV)
And said, "If you diligently heed the voice of the LORD your God and do what is right in His sight, give ear to His commandments and keep all His statutes, I will put none of

the diseases on you which I have brought on the Egyptians. For I *am* the LORD who heals you."

Serve the Lord and healing will be yours.
Exodus 23:25 New King James Version (NKJV)
"So you shall serve the LORD your God, and He will bless your bread and your water. And I will take sickness away from the midst of you.

God takes all sickness away from you.
Deuteronomy 7:15 New King James Version (NKJV)
And the LORD will take away from you all sickness, and will afflict you with none of the terrible diseases of Egypt which you have known, but will lay *them* on all those who hate you.

Obey all God's commandments and receive all His blessings.
Malachi 3:10 New King James Version (NKJV)
Bring all the tithes into the storehouse, That there may be food in My house, And try Me now in this," Says the LORD of hosts, "If I will not open for you the windows of heaven And pour out for you *such* blessing That *there will* not *be room* enough *to receive it.*

One of God's benefits is healing.

Psalms 103:1-5 New King James Version (NKJV)

Bless the LORD, O my soul; And all that is within me, *bless* His holy name! Bless the LORD, O my soul, And forget not all His benefits: Who forgives all your iniquities, Who heals all your diseases, Who redeems your life from destruction, Who crowns you with lovingkindness and tender mercies, Who satisfies your mouth with good *things,* So *that* your youth is renewed like the eagle's.

God's Word is healing.

Psalms 107:20 New King James Version (NKJV)

He sent His word and healed them, And delivered *them* from their destructions.

God wants you to live.

Psalms 118:17 New King James Version (NKJV)

I shall not die, but live, And declare the works of the LORD.

Choose to live. Be a fighter!

Deuteronomy 30:19 New King James Version (NKJV)

I call heaven and earth as witnesses today against you, *that* I have set before you life and death, blessing and cursing; therefore choose life, that both you and your descendants may live;

God will restore your health.

For I will restore health to you And heal you of your wounds,' says the LORD, 'Because they called you an outcast *saying:* "This *is* Zion; No one seeks her."'

Jeremiah 30:17

You will live a long life.
Psalms 91:16 New King James Version (NKJV)
With long life I will satisfy him, And show him My salvation."

Jesus bore your sins AND your sicknesses.
Isaiah 53:5 New King James Version (NKJV)
But He *was* wounded for our transgressions, *He was* bruised for our iniquities; The chastisement for our peace *was* upon Him, And by His stripes we are healed.

You can take authority over the sickness in your body.
Matthew 18:18 New King James Version (NKJV)
"Assuredly, I say to you, whatever you bind on earth will be bound in heaven, and whatever you loose on earth will be loosed in heaven.

Agree with someone for your healing.
Matthew 18:19 New King James Version (NKJV)
"Again I say to you that if two of you agree on earth concerning anything that they ask, it will be done for them by My Father in heaven.

What you say will make a difference.

Mark 11:22-23 New King James Version (NKJV)

So Jesus answered and said to them, "Have faith in God. For assuredly, I say to you, whoever says to this mountain, 'Be removed and be cast into the sea,' and does not doubt in his heart, but believes that those things he says will be done, he will have whatever he says.

Believe, and you will receive.

Mark 11:24 New King James Version (NKJV)

Therefore I say to you, whatever things you ask when you pray, believe that you receive *them*, and you will have *them*.

Plead your case to God.

Isaiah 43:25-26 New King James Version (NKJV)

"I, *even* I, *am* He who blots out your transgressions for My own sake; And I will not remember your sins. Put Me in remembrance; Let us contend together; State your *case*, that you may be acquitted.

Have someone lay hands on you for healing.

Mark 16:17-18 New King James Version (NKJV)

And these signs will follow those who believe: In My name they will cast out demons; they will speak with new tongues;

they will take up serpents; and if they drink anything deadly, it will by no means hurt them; they will lay hands on the sick, and they will recover."

Worship God.
John 9:31 New King James Version (NKJV)
Now we know that God does not hear sinners; but if anyone is a worshiper of God and does His will, He hears him.

The devil wants to kill you; God wants to heal you.
John 10:10 New King James Version (NKJV)
The thief does not come except to steal, and to kill, and to destroy. I have come that they may have life, and that they may have *it* more abundantly.

You are redeemed from the curse.
Galatians 3:13-14 New King James Version (NKJV)
Christ has redeemed us from the curse of the law, having become a curse for us (for it is written, "Cursed *is* everyone who hangs on a tree"), that the blessing of Abraham might come upon the Gentiles in Christ Jesus, that we might receive the promise of the Spirit through faith.

You will not waver in your faith.
Hebrews 10:23 New King James Version (NKJV)
Let us hold fast the confession of *our* hope without wavering, for He who promised *is* faithful.

You can have confidence in God and His Word.
Hebrews 10:35 New King James Version (NKJV)
Therefore do not cast away your confidence, which has great reward.

God's highest wish is for you to be well.
1 John 1:2 New King James Version (NKJV)
Beloved, I pray that you may prosper and be in health, just as your soul prospers.

Be anointed with oil by a Christian who believes in healing.
James 5:14-15 New King James Version (NKJV)
Is anyone among you sick? Let him call for the elders of the church, and let them pray over him, anointing him with oil in the name of the Lord. And the prayer of faith will save the sick, and the Lord will raise him up. And if he has committed sins, he will be forgiven.

Jesus Christ has never changed. What He did in the Bible, He will do for you today.

New King James Version (NKJV) Jesus Christ *is* the same yesterday, today, and forever.

Hebrews 13:8

Jesus has already paid the price for your healing.

Who Himself bore our sins in His own body on the tree, that we, having died to sins, might live for righteousness— by whose stripes you were healed.

1 Peter 2:24

New King James Version (NKJV)

You can find strength in God and His Word.
Joel 3:10 New King James Version (NKJV)
…Let the weak say, 'I *am* strong.'"

Be confident in your prayers.
1 John 5:14-15 New King James Version (NKJV)
Now this is the confidence that we have in Him, that if we ask anything according to His will, He hears us. And if we know that He hears us, whatever we ask, we know that we have the petitions that we have asked of Him.

God answers the prayers of those that keep His commandments.
1 John 3:21-22 New King James Version (NKJV)
Beloved, if our heart does not condemn us, we have confidence toward God. And whatever we ask we receive from Him, because we keep His commandments and do those things that are pleasing in His sight.
Fear is not of God. Rebuke it!

1Timothy 1:7 New King James Version (NKJV)
For God has not given us a spirit of fear, but of power and of love and of a sound mind.

Cast down those thoughts and imaginations that don't line up with the Word of God.

2 Corinthians 10:4-5 New King James Version (NKJV)

For the weapons of our warfare *are* not carnal but mighty in God for pulling down strongholds, casting down arguments and every high thing that exalts itself against the knowledge of God, bringing every thought into captivity to the obedience of Christ,

Be strong in the Lord's power. Put on His armor to fight for healing.

Ephesians 6:10-17 New King James Version (NKJV)

Finally, my brethren, be strong in the Lord and in the power of His might. Put on the whole armor of God, that you may be able to stand against the wiles of the devil. For we do not wrestle against flesh and blood, but against principalities, against powers, against the rulers of the darkness of this age, against spiritual *hosts* of wickedness in the heavenly *places.* Therefore take up the whole armor of God, that you may be able to withstand in the evil day, and having done all, to stand. Stand therefore, having girded your waist with truth, having put on the breastplate of righteousness, and having shod your feet with the preparation of the gospel of peace; above all, taking the shield of faith with which you will be able to quench all the fiery darts of the wicked one. And take the helmet of salvation, and the sword of the Spirit, which is the word of God;

Give testimony of your healing.
Revelations 12:11 New King James Version (NKJV)
And they overcame him by the blood of the Lamb and by the word of their testimony, and they did not love their lives to the death.

Your sickness will leave and not come back again.
Nahum 1:9 New King James Version (NKJV)
What do you conspire against the LORD? He will make an utter end *of it*. Affliction will not rise up a second time.

POISED

Chapter Twelve

PASTORS ON POINT INTERCEDING SPIRITUALLY EVERY DAY

If you are wondering why I only gave a brief dedication and acknowledgement to my pastors (who happens to be my biological sister and brother in love), it is because I could not say it all in those sections. I wanted to honor them and pen an entire chapter reverencing them.

Thus, I dedicate this chapter in P.O.I.S.E.D. by naming it "Pastors On point Interceding Spiritually Every Day."

Bellowing from every text message, the introduction to every phone call, the heading or closing of every email, and the greeting I got during every hospital visit, and even as I was greeted in person, were the famous scripted words of my sister, Dr. Bridget Hilliard:

"How are you today, healed woman of God?" You are the healed resisting sickness and disease.

This was consistently and emphatically spoken to me from the time of the diagnosis up until today. Spiritual leaders are important to your life. What is a spiritual leader? You may say they are our spiritual guru.

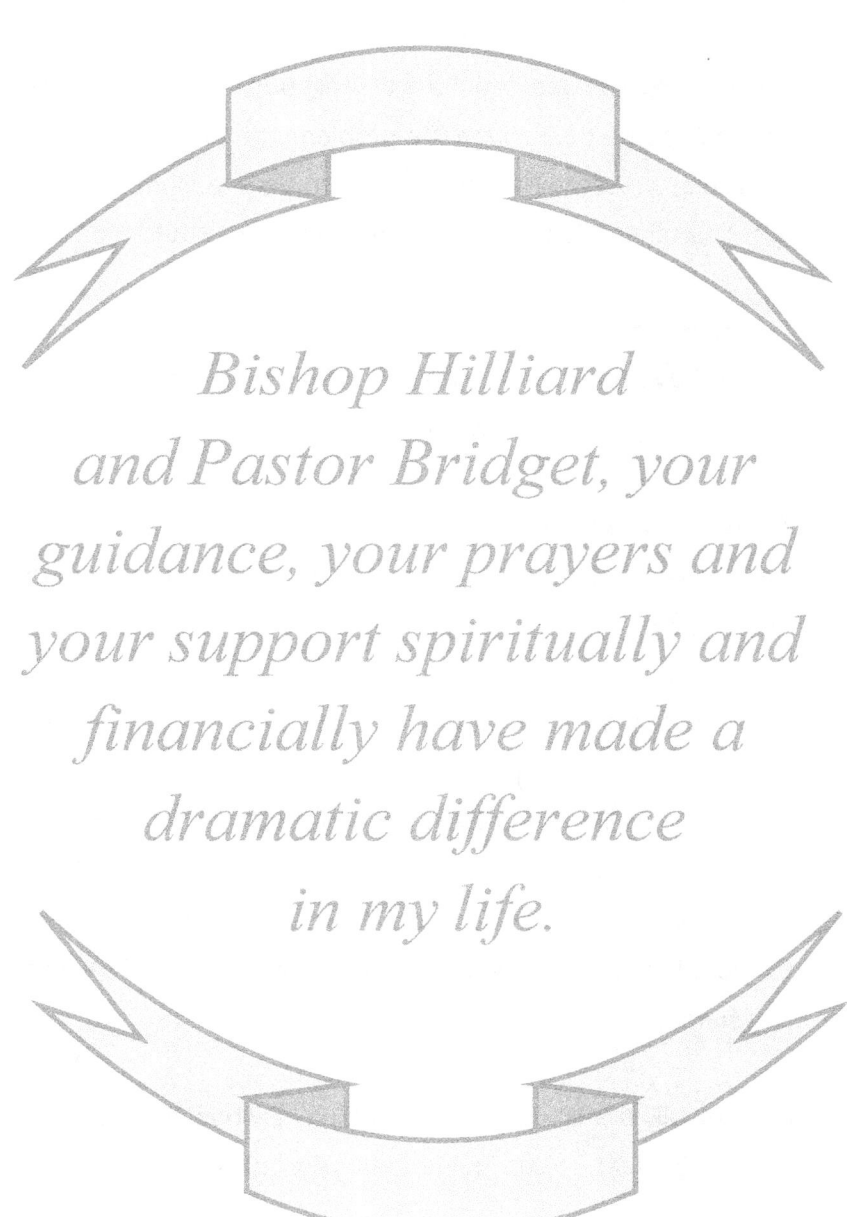

Bishop Hilliard and Pastor Bridget, your guidance, your prayers and your support spiritually and financially have made a dramatic difference in my life.

There is a saying, "Different strokes for different folks." Pastors, experts, and teachers on religious matters are ones who can guide us through the problems and trials of life. In the Bible, we see their ability to lead others to Christ as one gift. The other gift is to give guidance to your soul.

The book of Ephesians references the concerns a leader should have for the saint while also leading them to spiritual maturity and teaching them faith.

There is so much more than can be said about a spiritual leader. My spiritual leaders are included in that term and so much more.

Actually, let me introduce them to you.

Bishop I.V. Hilliard and Pastor Bridget Hilliard, I honor you both in this chapter. They are the dynamic duo behind New Light Christian Center Church World Outreach & Worship Centers Inc. Their passion is to teach faith and God's Word to a hurting and lost generation.

First of all, thank you for everything, Bishop Hilliard and Pastor Bridget. Your guidance, your prayers and your support spiritually and financially have made a dramatic difference in my life.

One evening, while sitting in my recliner, I thought, "Wow, I need to have Bishop pray over some oil for me." Afterwards, I sent the oil back with one of the ladies that worked for them. A few weeks later, I asked for the oil back, but did not get it. I thought it may have been given to someone else or that perhaps Bishop Hilliard had not gotten the oil.

I got on the phone and personally called about the oil and Bishop said, "I'm not through praying over it yet." A month passed, and still no oil. Each time I asked, Bishop would say, "I'm still praying over your oil." He would take the oil and pray over it each day. Thank God for his commitment.

Finally, after six weeks, I got the oil back. Once I had the oil in my hand, I would take it and rub it on my legs every day. You see, at this time I was on a walker and could not move without help and assistance. So I bathe my legs in this oil.

One day, Bishop Hilliard sent me a message to wiggle my toes. Then he sent me another message: "Swing one foot out the bed, then the other."

Eventually, my legs began to move more and more. I had to stop driving for a period of time because I could not move my legs fast enough to accelerate and brake properly. But as I continuously use the oil, I was eventually able to start driving again.

I will never forget New Year's Eve 2013. I was in the hospital and was told I would be there a few more days. I called Dr. Bridget and said I wanted to be at the service. In 28 years, I had never missed a New Year's Eve service.

Dr. Bridget got in agreement with me and also shared with Bishop Hilliard how I wanted to be at that service. Later that day, one of the nurses came in and said, "I don't know what changed, but they just said you can be discharged!" **But God!!!**

I called my sister, Andrea, to pick me up, and thank God the service didn't start until 9 p.m., because they took their time about discharging me. Finally, I got home just in time to make it to service that night. When Bishop Hilliard was told that I had been released, he sent me a message that said, "Press your way to service tonight. I will pray for you."

I pressed my way, and Bishop did indeed pray for me. He walked off and then turned back and grabbed me and said, "You shall live and not die." That was a turning point in my life.

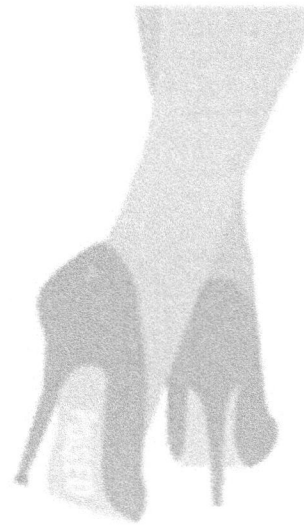

At one point, I had been to doctor after doctor and felt like the woman in the Bible with the issue of blood, because it seemed that there was no relief. But when Bishop spoke that word, my spirit leaped and my faith was reignited.

That hit my spirit very hard, and it gave me hope to push pass the pain and stay poised.

At one point, I had been to doctor after doctor and felt like the woman in the Bible with the issue of blood, because it seemed that there was no relief. But when Bishop spoke that word, my spirit leaped and my faith was reignited.

The pain of lupus and the flares are so severe sometimes that you just need a word from the prophet to keep pushing. This is what I received this night!

GET UP!
FIX UP!
LOOK UP!

Chapter Thirteen

BUT YOU DON'T LOOK SICK...

What does sick look like?

Because I don't have an amputation of some sort, it leaves a question in the mind of the person addressing the issue or making the statement that I don't look sick. People can really be insensitive, uncaring, or just simply don't understand what you are going through while you're living with lupus.

Get educated on the matter. Any chronic illness is a life-altering experience. Sometimes the lack of understanding from others can be just as painful as the physical pain itself.

I dislike that people don't understand and don't know how lupus affects you daily. It amazes me that people jump to assumptions, such as that you are lazy, flaky, or a hypochondriac.

One of my friends explained it like this: "The piranhas are loose inside your system." My health is unpredictable. There are episodes known as pain cycles, and though you may not see a single outward sign of pain, the pain that's raging on the inside can be unbearable. Thank God my mom taught me that no matter what I was going through, I should not ever go out looking as if something was wrong. She taught us to always look your best when you leave your house. Being poised is a must. There really is a connection to the saying, "Get up, fix up." You will feel better and then you can look up.

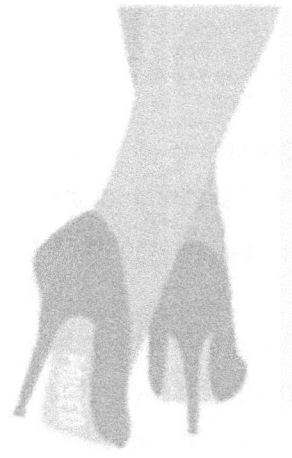

The one hurtful statement that always caused me to gasp was, "Are you really in that much pain?" or, "Is it really that bad?"

Lupus and any other chronic illness will not always be obvious when you look at someone. Because of this, family and friends struggle with the severity of the symptoms: achy muscles, painful arthritis, extreme fatigue, low-grade fever, pain fluctuations, swelling and inflammation, and surprise attacks that show up like an uninvited guest at your front door and may result in being hospitalized.

The pain is real, even though I don't look sick (and I never will look sick, because of what was embedded in me as a child). I am going to always look my best, even when I'm not feeling my best, but please note that the pain is real.

The one hurtful statement that always caused me to gasp was, "Are you really in that much pain?" or, "Is it really that bad?" Usually, the only indication you might have that someone is having an episode is a frown that may appear on their face if they move or try to shift their posture.

Typically, a person dealing with lupus has had to put forth more effort than otherwise to actually look the way they do. Oftentimes, they have had to cover up because of rashes that will not heal.

I once had a rash on my body that would not heal for a year. It took me extra time and effort to make sure the rash was not visible and thus distracting to others. I had to use makeup to cover up breakouts, scars, infections, etc.

Sometimes I had to wear extra clothing to camouflage certain disorders. A pale complexion almost always accompanies lupus and other chronic illnesses, so I had to do extra to enhance my appearance and look well.

I would have my own dress up days where I would go through a full regimen just to walk to my mailbox. (By the way, it took hours to make myself look well during that time.)

Added skepticism to what I was going through was not welcomed. When I had done everything right and still feel all wrong, I still had to be in a poised position. To all the individuals on Facebook that would make ugly comments as to why I took so many selfies, I did that because I was encouraging myself. Even a woman who is dealing with a chronic illness is still a beautiful woman, and I find strength in appearing beautiful.

Let me educate those of you in the medical field as well on an issue that would send me into orbit.

When I would go to the doctor or the hospital, I would still put on my lip gloss, my earrings, and my matching ballerina shoes. But again, because I didn't look sick, they would asked the infamous question: "On a scale of 1-10, how bad is your pain?" Many times, I would say, "22." That was my standard to throw them off, but also send the message that you cannot equate the pain I'm going through on the same scale as someone who had a minor headache. Those little faces on the pain chart don't do justice to a person dealing with episodes of lupus. Pain and fatigue is different for each person. Even lupus patients have varying degrees of pain.

I have the determination to be poised, to defeat this disease, and to live by the principals taught to me by my mother, Jewell. She taught me to confess the Word over my body daily, therefore, I won't ever look sick. I am poised, positioned, and predestined for greatness. I am unapologetically poised.

Again, though one may not look sick, lupus is very painful and it can be very exhausting. Patients may experience a wide range of symptoms, including feeling as though you have the flu everyday of your life. It is a discomfort you cannot even imagine, and lupus affects each patient differently. It can bring many different emotions: resentment, fear, and even depression. Lupus patients need lots of help, as the illness greatly weakens the immune system.

Please take the time to get educated on what you or your loved one is dealing with when diagnosed with lupus or any autoimmune disease.

POWER, ABILITY AND INFLUENCE

Chapter Fourteen

DYNAMIC DUO TIMES TWO

After 42 years of diligence in a career that I loved dearly, I had to step away and regain my strength. The sudden emotional shift and change in personality was a result of having a very difficult time. I have the propensity to push pass the pain of lupus and be poised, therefore, I have now learned new coping skills.

For those battling lupus, you can become emotional from out of nowhere when you don't fully realize what's going on with you from day to day. You have a sense of loss, you tend to feel embarrassed, and you feel afraid.

The dynamic duo x2:
My little sister, Andrea (the baby of the Harrison clan).

Andrea never wanted me to be in pain. She did whatever necessary to try to relieve it; however, there were days when not even the Prednisone or Toroidal shots would help. Even so, she made sure she did whatever it took to keep me poised.

Whatever she had to do after work each day never happened. I became her priority during this time, and she was my caretaker. Thanks, Andrea, for devoting all your spare time to nurturing me back to health.

Latonya Mayes (my Godchild's mom): You have been my "Do I need to come, girl?" You rock! Not one time did I call without you saying, "What do you need?" or "Do I need to come?" Challenging times can be so much better when you have a support system like these two. Tonya was going to make it happen no matter what the cost. I remember one day she brought her whole family to make it happen for me.

There are just no words for this; "Thanks" is close, but does not touch the surface. Here is a list of some of the many things I am grateful for that can be summed up as having my every earthly desire met: you have been my drivers, my specific-restaurant- request-goers, my organizers and thought processors during my move, my cooks, my whatever-I-needed buddies.

Thanks, ladies. You were there for me like the plastic crate you have when you go through hurricane season -- my survivor kits with everything needed to make it through that season. You ladies were always just a phone call away. When I was too weary to walk, lift, or even dress myself, you ladies were there. Love you to the moon and back.

Pastor Renee Hornbuckle and Pastor Quett Easter are true servants of God. What can be said about these two ladies? When it was so dark that I couldn't see my hand in front of me, you ladies were my beam of light.

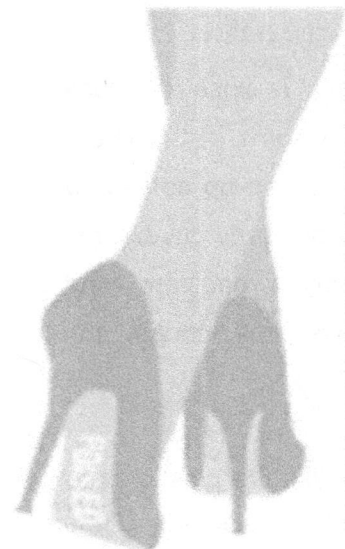

The pain was so Severe that I could barely move around and I could not think clearly. I felt as if I was drowning and could not breathe. But again, God had a ram in the bush.

If the pain or flare-ups from lupus were not enough, I now had to make a major decision to move from my home that I had grown used to. I felt secure and comfortable there, but I was blindsided. You see, I could no longer pay my bills or keep up with the demands of the household. It was devastating.

The pain was so severe that I could barely move around and I could not think clearly. I felt as if I was drowning and could not breathe. But once again, God had a ram in the bush.

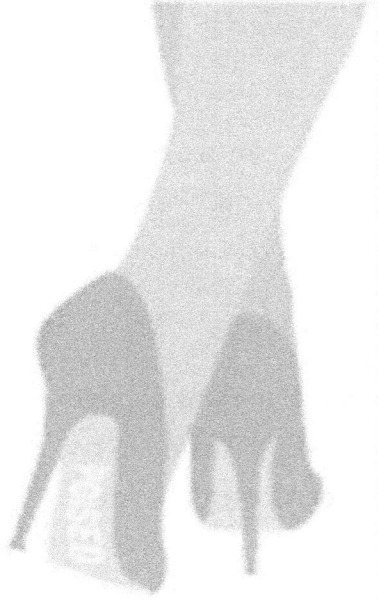

You see, I had to downsize, find a new place to live, get medical attention and see a therapist, and find lots of help. I could not think through any of this on my own and was at a state of not functioning normally.

Pastor Renee Hornbuckle and Pastor Quett Easter, I will never be able to say thank you enough. Your friendship and love is past my comprehension. A full-time Senior Pastor and her assistant dropped everything in Dallas, Texas, to move in with me for weeks to help me make this transition.

You see, I had to downsize, find a new place to live, get medical attention and see a therapist, and find lots of help. I could not think through any of this on my own and was at a state of not functioning normally.

Pastor Renee and Pastor Quett came, moved me, helped me downsize, set up my new living quarters, put everything in order, and made sure I was comfortable and functioning well for the journey ahead.

Andrea and Tonya were there every step of the way as well. The dynamic duo times two. You ladies rock. There are no words adequate enough to say thanks for caring for my well-being.

Chapter Fifteen

UNTIL YOU HAVE WALKED A MILE IN MY SHOES

On July 15, 2015, I went to the doctor because of pain in my lower stomach. The pain was so bad I had to hold the bottom of my stomach to walk comfortably. It was determined that this may be a severe bladder infection or part of a flare-up.

While sitting there, waiting for the doctor, I begin to jot a few items down on a piece of paper. As my doctor came in and out of the room, she asked, "What are you doing; writing down what you want to tell me?"

I said, "No; I'm actually writing down my thoughts to insert in my book."

Dr. Bullard said, "You are writing a book?" I replied, "Yes." "Great!" she said. Then the doctor turned to me and said, "Please include the journey of your disease and what you go through on a daily basis. Please explain thoroughly for those who don't understand or even care to understand."

She went on to say how the disease affects many African-American women, but they have very little knowledge about lupus and don't try to gain the proper knowledge needed. Research shows that lupus is two to three times more prevalent in woman of color.

Dr. Bullard went on to say that when people don't understand what you are dealing with and don't understand the unpredictable symptoms, your words to them should be, "Until you've walked a mile in my shoes, then don't judge me."

People can be harsh and say all kinds of things when they don't understand. They tend to say, "You don't look sick," or "Are you in pain today?" when, in fact, you are in pain most days.

She went on to say many times that people do mean well, but are really destroyed for a lack of knowledge. It just all seems to come out wrong sometimes. From that, this chapter was born.

Until You Have Walked a Mile in My Shoes

The first thing that a person must realize is that when you have been as active as I was and now are no longer at that same activity level, you did not intentionally give up the activities that you were once so used to.

Others must have a desire to learn what's really going on with the disease. The patient only wants your support. Living with the disease and/or debilitating factors is very hard when there is lack of understanding. Let me share what one encounters.

Because a person like me was taught from childhood to get up, fix up, and look up, others find themselves struggling to believe their limitations. We look at the person and say, "Oh, she looks fine," yet we disregard what they say when things like this are voiced:

1. No, I can't; my body won't let me today.
2. I'm very fatigued and walking a distance is not good for me today.
3. I can't fold clothes today.
4. Shopping and walking is certainly out for me today.
5. I have been in the bed all day.
6. I have been in pain for days.
7. It is hard for me to open this water bottle.
8. I'm unable to bend to pick something off the floor.
9. My feet are swollen today.
10. I have a fever and sore throat right now.
11. I have been in pain for three days now.
12. I'm cold and need a blanket.
13. My eyes are bloodshot.
14. Please understand that if I stand for 5 minutes, it doesn't mean that I can stand for 10.
15. Buttons are out of the question.

Most responses will be, "But I just saw you at the function yesterday." Or, "You were fine this morning; how can that be?" It's because of the unpredictability of the disease.

To anyone with no knowledge about lupus, it is incomprehensible! If we don't take the time to educate our family and friends about the disease, they make statements like, "She's lazy," "It can't be that bad," "She needs to get it together," or even, "I think she is faking because I saw her moving around yesterday."

Although a person's pain may not always be visible, and visible symptoms may not appear on the onset of looking at them, *the disease is real.* This chapter will bring to the forefront the *reality for you* as family members and friends to truly understand the difficulties and challenges that come with lupus.

1. There were days when I ached all over.
2. I had to deal with pain spasm in the back of my legs.
3. My fingers would cramp up in the middle of a task.
4. I have slept with an electric blanket in Houston, Texas in the months of May, June, and July.
5. My blood pressure stayed at 220/180 for days.

6. Allergies popped up out of nowhere. I could eat something one day without a reaction, and then eat that same thing the next day and land in the hospital.
7. You never know what part of the body will flare up.
8. Lupus can put you to bed in an instant. You may have a short trip to the grocery store and, afterwards, be in bed for days.
9. You can be feeling fine and, an hour later, be unable to move due to joint pain.
10. Activities and events are never easy to plan.
11. Some conditions are persistent and long-lasting.
12. Shortness of breath may occur when you walk from your bed to the bathroom.
13. If you stand to cook a meal, it is difficult to clean the kitchen afterwards.
14. You have to pick what task you will perform each day. Doing what you used to do is no longer something that can be accomplished in one day.
15. Things change: you can no longer fulfill the roles and duties you were once able to fulfill.

These very symptoms can cause you loss of employment, loss of wages, and require major adjustments in your life.

Chapter Sixteen

I'M ON THE FRONT PEW

The most devastating statements made to me through my journey were:

1. "You mean you have preachers all around you, and your family is in ministry, and they haven't prayed this off of you? Are you still really dealing with this, or are you faking?"

2. "In a church service, the pastor targets you consistently and say you need to stand. You are being disobedient. Are you just gonna ignore my command? See, it's people like you that want a blessing and won't get one, because you won't do something as simple as stand when I ask you."

In truth, it took every ounce of my energy to get here today. My joints are so inflamed and in pain that I really won't be able to get up and down each time. It's a struggle. At the end of the service, when it is time to dismiss, even then it will take me a minute to get myself together, stand, and be able to move forward. Though going at my own pace, I will be poised.

Chapter Seventeen

POISED

P.O.I.S.E.D.: Positioned to Overcome Illness, Stabilizing my Equilibrium towards Destiny.

Anyone who knows me knows that when I step out, I'm going to be jazzy, matching, color-coordinated, and accessorized.

Poised in my own lane.

It could take me up to three hours to ready my appearance because of dealing with sore joints, a fatigued body, and being very careful not to overexert my heart. I have to carefully plan my strategies. I typically would have spent hours the previous night putting together my outfit and making sure everything was within reach.

Usually, I had to start by getting something in my system: fruit, lemon water, or a small bowl of oatmeal. I would always make sure a chair to sit on was available for me in between each task. This is a simple task that may take 20 minutes for the average person, but it is not as easy for me.

You have 100 marbles of energy to start your day and do all of the tasks you need to do that day. Well, my day would start off with maybe 10 marbles, and I still had to accomplish all of my daily duties. Lupus drained my energy.

When deciding on lunch, I always had to be conscious of what and how much I ate. Raw vegetables were a major part of my recovery.

In addition, I followed a daily regimen of confessions according to the Word of God. The first thing out of my mouth every morning was, "Thank you, Holy Spirit, for comforting me all through the night and waking me up to see a brand new day. Thank you for your mercies that are new every morning. Great is thy faithfulness."

The second thing I would do was say, "I am the healed, resisting sickness and disease." Next, "He sent His word to heal me and deliver me from destruction."

At this point, I would go through a series of confessions:

"With long life he satisfies me and shows me his salvation." —Psalm 91:6

"Christ bore our sickness on the tree and by his stripes we were healed." —Isaiah 53:5

"Surely he bore our griefs on the tree." —Isaiah 53:4

"I shall live and not die and declare the works of the Lord." — Psalm 188:17

I later added to my confessions a term I learned from Apostle JoAnn Long, Pastor of New Life Believers Church (Chicago,

Illinois) as she spoke at the 2015 "Women Who Win" Conference. During her testimony, she said she would say, "I don't want it." It's a short, simple phrase, but very powerful. I would say this whenever I felt pain in my body.

"I Don't Want It."

Chapter Eighteen

LUPUS & MY FAITH

I would be remiss if I did not include this chapter in my book, which is about how to conquer the monster with the words of my mouth and living by principles that the Word of God teaches.

This is my own testimony. I'm not giving advice to your symptoms, nor am I giving out medical advice. I am not claiming it as a panacea. This is simply the regiment that kept me afloat while I endured the pain.

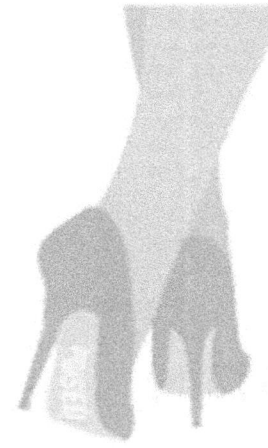

I thank God for His continuous healing power.

POISED 101

Lupus is such a debilitating disease that I needed more than doctors and medicine alone. I didn't have to turn to the Word of God, as the saying goes, as I was already acquainted with and plugged into God's promises and His blueprint for us.

As I previously stated in my acknowledgements, I thank God for His continuous healing power. I thank Him for His abundant grace and new mercies every morning. Because of my dependency on him, I am able to be P.O.I.S.E.D.

Chapter Nineteen

TIPS, HINTS, & INSIGHT

As stated in previous chapters, lupus can be quite challenging. Symptoms can vary and there can be a fairly wide range. The pain can be from mild to severe at any given time.

Again, it is so hard to plan for events and activities when struggling with lupus. For impact's sake, I will list some of the common symptoms.

- Pain
- Swelling of joints
- Fatigue
- High blood pressure
- Fever
- Headaches
- Sensitivity to weather
- Weight loss
- Hair loss
- Movement restrictions

I have come to realize that the flare-ups caused by lupus can be more horrendous than the actual illness.

It has been said that there is no cure for lupus; however, you can live and not die—and even succeed and be "poised."

As a person being challenged with lupus, I would like to give a few practical tips to friends and family. To gain insight on what you and/or your family members are dealing with, you must:

1. Renew your mind.
2. Confess the Word over yourself and/or your loved one.
3. Take courage.
4. Have a health regimen.
5. Become very interactive and conversational with your doctors.
6. Be determined to stay poised.
7. Get knowledge and education about lupus.
8. Accept help and support from those who offer it to you.
9. Keep details of symptoms and episodes in a diary.
10. Above all, stand and do not allow lupus to identify you.

One of the infamous phrases that I have grown to dislike is, "If you need me, call me." I think we often say that phrase to be kind or just out of duty. That phrase is taken as literal by those with a chronic illness, so if you do, in fact, throw it out there, be ready to follow through with your promise.

During my challenging time, I was crushed because I called a dear friend and asked for help, but the response I got was, "You need me do that now?" From two different people on two different occasions, the other answer I got was, "Oh, no, I can't."

(The average person going through a debilitating illness will not call you, but I did because I was invited to do so.)

The other phrase you shouldn't use unless you really mean it is, "Call me any time." Ninety-nine percent of people who say that don't mean it.

When the pain hits or your heart starts beating too rapidly at 2 or 3 a.m., you really can't wait until the 9 a.m. – 9 p.m. time frame to call. Usually, if someone calls you at a weird time frame, it's because they are in need. Pick up the phone.

Since the average person is not going to call because of shame (not wanting to bother anyone or because they are in too much pain and disgust), let me give some suggestions for helping out someone with a chronic illness.

Dealing with lupus, as said, can be very painful. It becomes hard for someone with lupus to perform normal household duties, so don't wait for them to ask. There is always something to do.

In your leisure time, go by and wash a load of clothes for them. Empty the garbage, dust, or just pick things up and put them back in place. Cook a healthy meal for them, but if you're not a cook, stop at the store and pick up fresh fruit, juice, soup, salad; anything easy for them to get to. If you can't do that, there are many places that deliver various items. Two of my favorite are Greenling online and Squeezed online (fresh).

Luby's is always a good choice to stop and pick up a meal. In addition, remember that they often experience pain along with fatigue, making it hard for them to do grocery shopping. Pick up a few things when you are out for yourself and take it to them. A basket filled with items and a nice bow will be so appreciated.

Here are some basket ideas:

1. Snack basket
Fill this basket with healthy bars, water, fruit, nuts, popcorn, etc. These are only suggestions; you can always add more or delete.

2. Toiletry basket

Fill this with wipes, soap, mouthwash, toothpaste, toilet tissue, washcloths, lotion, Vaseline, deodorant, cotton balls, Benadryl, Ibuprofen, etc. Again, these are only suggestions; you can add more or delete. For this one, you would want to be specific on brands and what the person can use. Ask before you buy. Know that some individuals may have allergic reactions or their skin maybe sensitive to certain things that everyone else uses.

3. Household needs basket

Fill this with dishwashing liquid, detergent, fabric softener, Downey, paper towels, air freshener, etc. Pods are a lifesaver to a person dealing with joint pain. (Again, these are only suggestions; you can add more or delete.)

Personally, I would have welcomed any of these items. I could never run out of Witch Hazel. I would have given anything for someone to have picked me up a bottle or two on those days when I was unable to make it to the store. (Tip: Walmart yellow brand label is the cheapest on the market.)

Help with rides to the doctor's office.

Lupus has changed the lifestyle that the person is accustomed to; loss of work, loss of finances, loss of home, etc. could all have resulted from this chronic illness.

Doctor bills are enormous and meds are not that cheap, either. Even if someone has insurance and/or disability benefits, it is never enough to take care of all the essentials, so there are many times when they do without.

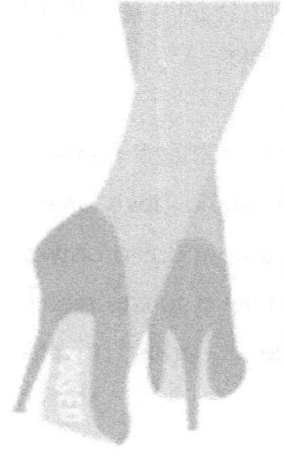

"If you need me, call me." A person with lupus needs constant support in one way or another. The disease in itself is very complicated.

Gift cards are always welcome. Cash is even better. Five or ten dollars is a wealth to someone who has been standing for healing for a period of time.

If the person living with lupus is single, agree to take their vehicle and gas it up or have it detailed for them. Those are tasks that take a lot of energy and are always welcomed. The game of finding the right medication can be very frustrating. Many times, some meds don't work, and changing them periodically may be necessary. This can be costly.

Now you know to be very careful when you say, "If you need me, call me." A person with lupus needs constant support in one way or another. The disease in itself is very complicated. A group of people in your life with various influence is much needed. As a believer, our dependence is on God. However, we need family and friends to use their power, ability, and influence on our behalf. When you have a strong support system, it helps you better navigate your way through the difficult times.

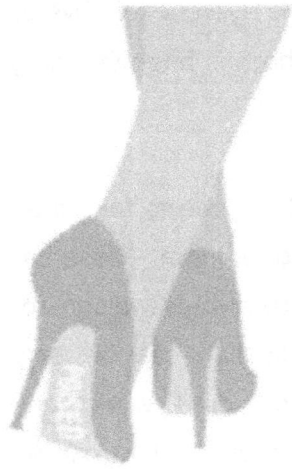

Lupus can trigger all kinds of emotions. Don't get offended over simple responses. Moods shift greatly with this disease.

I cannot stress enough that family and friends must be that support. Not everything going on may be verbalized by the person dealing with lupus.

Hopefully, as I've walked this journey, you, the reader, have gained some valuable insight. We need others as support on this journey. So you may want to change what you say to, "How can I be of service to you today?"

Another insight…

Lupus can trigger all kinds of emotions. Don't get offended over simple responses. Moods shift greatly with this disease. Many times, we, the lupus patient, do not want to be a burden; after all, this may have been going on for months or even years. Emotional times are real when we experience pain. Don't take it personally and know that it's not directed towards you. We're all doing the best that we can do.

Chapter Twenty

GRATITUDE MOMENTS

I am most grateful to my primary doctor, Dr. A. Michelle Bullard. Words are not adequate to describe your caring for my well-being. I am thankful not only for your medical advice, but also because I knew when I stepped through your doors I would get a confession of faith and prayer. When I wasn't able to lift a finger to stand on my own, you nurtured me back to a state of health to keep being poised.

I am also most grateful to Ms. Gwen Berry, who was there on the scene when I had the worst scare of my entire life. This is when my heart was racing and out of control. It literally had to be stopped and restarted, and you were there praying in the Holy Ghost, covering me in prayer, my body and my thoughts. Because of your presence, I was able to stay poised.

Fear will literally grab you by the throat, cut off your circulation, and have you grasping for breath. The news was unbelievable, and my world changed in an instant.

Chapter Twenty One

A MESSAGE OF HOPE

Although there is no known medical cure for lupus, there is hope. One of the places of hope is to have hope and remember that lupus may have hurt my feelings, but it didn't hurt my faith. In order to stand and be poised, you must have a regimen of faith. Stay in the race. Never give up, because God rewards your faith and diligence.

Remember, disease is tamed when I say HIS name.

Lupus and any other chronic disease can be managed with:

- A regimen of treatment from your doctor
- A regimen of faith
- A regimen of belief
- A regimen of healthy eating
- A regimen of the Word (faith comes by hearing)
- A regimen of confessions

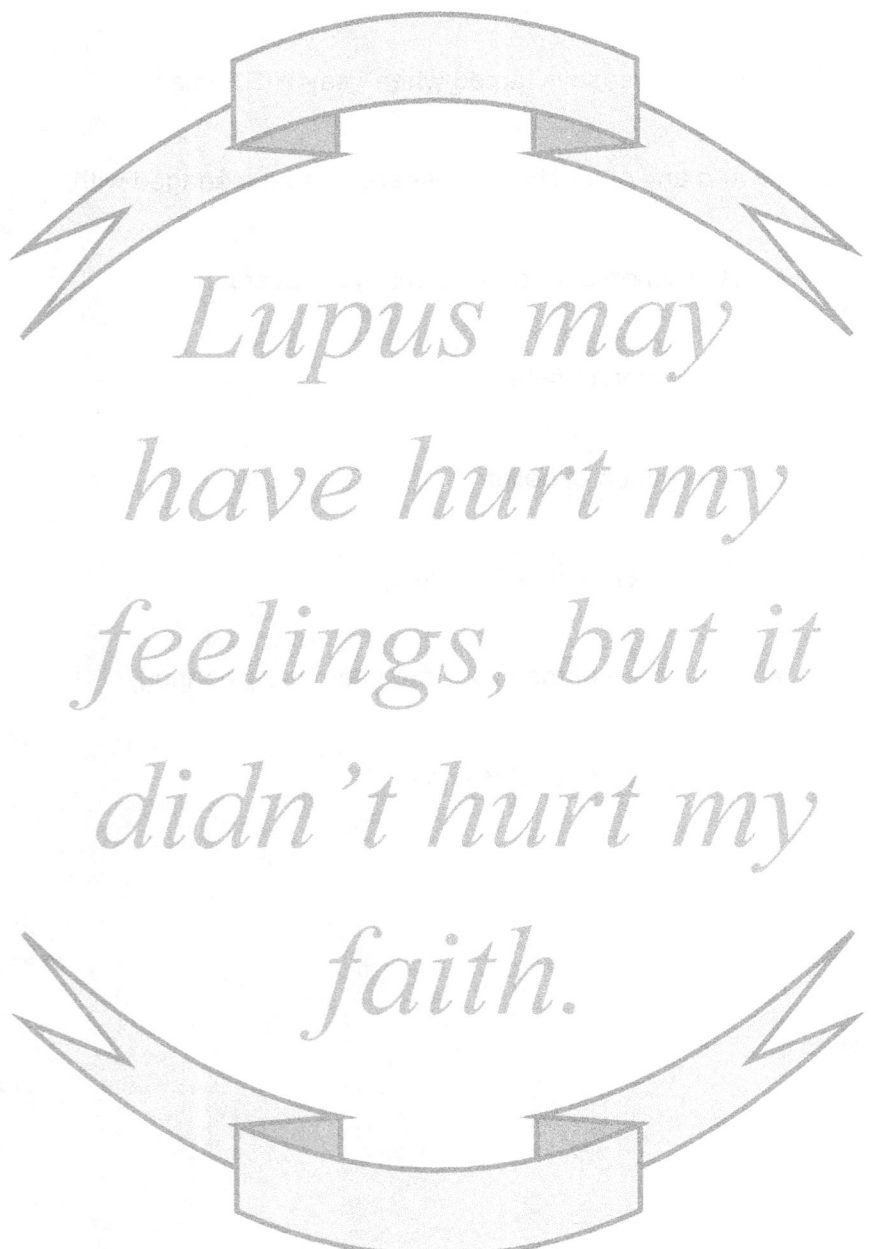

Lupus may have hurt my feelings, but it didn't hurt my faith.

Wytress Mitchell

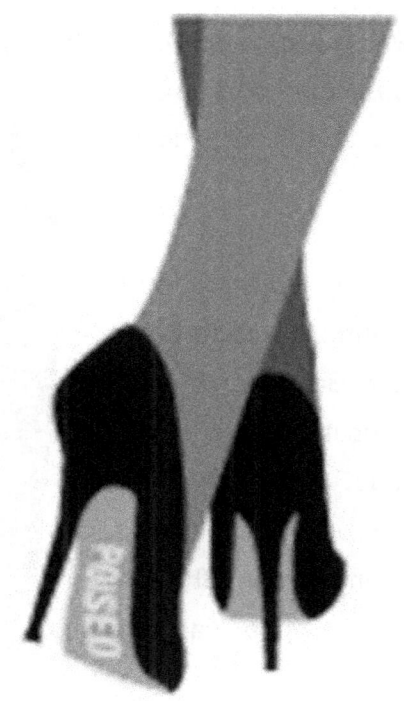

About the Author

Wytress Mitchell is an author, educator, and minister who is a survivor living with lupus. She was born and raised in Houston, Texas, and is the oldest of four siblings.

Educated in the Houston public school system through grade twelve, Wytress holds a Bachelor of Arts in Elementary Education from Huston-Tillotson College, and a Masters of Arts from the University of Phoenix in Curriculum and Instruction. She is a member of the Alpha Kappa Alpha Sorority.

Wytress gave 42 years of her life to educate young minds in public, charter, and Christian schools. She contributes many of her lovely qualities that were inherited from her mother, Jewell Harrison, who has gone to be with the Lord but instilled much of who Wytress is today. In fact, part of this book was birthed out of early wisdom and knowledge that she drew from her mother. Being "poised" is something Wytress learned early in her youth, thus contributing to the title of her new book and ministry.

Wytress has served in ministry most of her life and is presently a Minister in good standing at New Light Christian Church, where she has been a member for 28+ years. She serves in several areas of excellence ministry, and is also an intercessor. Wytress also serves in a leadership capacity for several ministries in Houston and the surrounding areas.

Having received several life coach certifications, along with other recognitions through the educational field, Wytress has conducted numerous workshops in many different areas of ministry and education. She is known for her expertise in taking children that cannot read and write to the next level of being able to do so.

Wytress is also known as a connector. She is well known for knowing many personalities and can generally point you in the right direction of who you need to connect with.

Recently, Wytress has stepped forward to join the team of those who speak for lupus awareness.

Wytress' new release is to give insight to those who may not fully understand one dealing with an autoimmune disease. No matter what transition you have been through, you can still be "poised."

Wytress is the mother of three children and grandmother of four.

www.ingramcontent.com/pod-product-compliance
Lightning Source LLC
Chambersburg PA
CBHW061302110426
42742CB00012BA/2024